W9-COU-806

The
Golden Buddha
Changing Masks

Essays on the Spiritual Dimension of Acting

by
Mark Olsen

GATEWAYS/IDHHB PUBLISHING

This book is dedicated to my teachers who have provoked, guided, and inspired me to keep searching. It is further dedicated to my workmate, partner and wife, Jane, whose love and support gave me the courage to continue writing.

Copyright ©1989 by Gateways
All Rights Reserved. Printed in the U.S.A.
First Printing.

Published by:
GATEWAYS / IDHHB, INC.
PO Box 370
Nevada City, CA 95959
(916) 477-1116

No part of this publication may be reproduced or transmitted in any form or by any means, electronic or mechanical, including photocopy, recording, or any information storage and retrieval system now known or to be invented, without permission in writing from the copyright holder, except by a reviewer who wishes to quote brief passages in connection with a review written for inclusion in a magazine, newspaper, or broadcast.

Library of Congress Cataloging in Publication Data
Olsen, Mark, 1954-
    The Golden buddha changing masks : essays on
the spiritual dimension of acting / by Mark Olsen
        p. cm.
    Includes bibliographical references and index.
    ISBN 0-89556-083-6. -- ISBN 0-89556-058-5 (pbk.) : $12.50
    1. Acting. 2. Spiritual life. I. Title.
PN2071.P78047 1989
792'.028--dc20   89-1409
                                                          CIP

TABLE OF CONTENTS

PREFACE

In *The Golden Buddha Changing Masks,* Mark Olsen asks "Why should inspiration and growth in the spiritual dimension be relegated only to poets, musicians, painters, and dancers? The actor, too, has the right and the means to enter through the mysterious gates and struggle to awaken."

In this ground-breaking and stimulating book, the author reminds us of the spiritual longings that gave rise to the craft of acting in the distant past; he skillfully details how the spiritual path to awakening parallels, in important aspects, the path of the actor as he prepares his body, voice, intellect and spirit for the practice of his craft. In an astonishing new look at Stanislavski, Olsen uncovers the strong influence of the perennial wisdom traditions, including the Hindu, on the man who formulated the most influential acting theories of the modern Western theater.

Above all, in an era in which mass entertainment and commercial necessity seem at times to have all but obliterated the spiritual practice and ritual that brought the theater to life, Mark Olsen reminds actors and people of the theater of who we really are, and what we may yet become, if we have sufficient discipline and courage.

This book is sure to be greeted with joy and relief that, at last, we have been reminded of the "road less travelled" that was there all along, waiting to be reclaimed by a new generation of artists.

For those eager to start the journey, the book is full of practical exercises and suggestions for beginning, one step at a time, to reconnect their artistic energies to the ancient sources of power and joy.

Ruby Allen, Ph.D.
Director of Voice and Speech Training
The Florida State University/
Asolo Conservatory of Professional Actor Training

INTRODUCTION

There are no accidents. It is no accident that I have written this book and it is no accident that you are reading it. This book has come to you because you are in some way linked with the performing arts and have also been exposed to one or more facets of the spiritual quest. Or perhaps you are a student in a religious tradition, involved in one of the myriad paths toward self-realization, enlightenment, or whatever term you wish to use depicting an evolved state of awareness, and hoping to further your knowledge. Perhaps, like me, you confess to elements of both.

Whatever the circumstances, it is my wish that this book may provide you with fresh perspectives and clarity in your search.

I began writing this book because I realized that it *must* be written. I had seen too many "casualty cases" and had undergone too much struggle to let my discoveries rest within me.

I realize that inevitably, for some, one or more of the essays in this book will seem simplistic; while for others, each one will be fresh and profoundly important. Regardless of the level you have reached in your quest, I urge you to read the text slowly and carefully and to read only when you are completely alert.

Many aspects of the book are written on several levels at once, and you will need patience and a degree of contemplative penetration to grasp them fully. Even if you get confused or you sense that you have heard it all before—slow down and read with new eyes. You will be rewarded with astonishing and unexpected insights.

As a child, I was exposed to many religious teachings. I witnessed American Indian rituals, and had my share of visions, voices, and bumps in the night. As I grew older, the theatre became an outlet for creative energy and a much-needed grounding device. It was in the world of theatre that I began to make some sense of the world outside and to come to grips with the enormous world within me.

Although I was regarded highly as a speaking actor in college, I felt my true calling to be in the world of mime. I had a natural flair for it and pursued training at every opportunity.

Maybe it was the silence of the art form, or maybe it was just my particular fate at the time, but for whatever reason, I was continuously encountering teachings and masters from many spiritual traditions. There were moments of understanding so profound as to shake my body to the toes and there were moments, all too often I'm afraid, when I was locked in a confused anguish—feeling lost and unbearably alone.

As one might expect, I discovered that this state of knowing/not-knowing fed nicely into my blossoming artistry. I therefore maintained an avid involvement in spiritual work.

Eventually, I had the good fortune to perform and tour as a member of the internationally acclaimed mime/mask show, Mummenschanz. The tour exposed me to a number of new cultures, ideas, and experiences, punctuated time and again by meetings with profound spiritual teachers. Gradually, almost imperceptibly, I began to detach myself from my earlier theatrical aspirations and to delve deeper and deeper into spiritual matters.

The further I delved, the further I seemed to be from anything resembling the acting profession. Even when I wanted to establish myself and work in the mainstream acting scene, it was nearly impossible—but not because of the usual reasons. The fact was, I had seen too much: Indians commanding the clouds to rain, a teacher singing from the heart and the smell of roses permeating the room, a UFO sighting, profound shamanistic healing experiences, deep meditative insights, the Golden Buddha manifesting in my dreams, teachers with true realization emanating from their being, mind-boggling synchronicity, and visions so astounding as to shatter my normal reality. Theatre simply paled by comparison.

However, as the glittering aspects of my quest began to settle into a total shape, not only did they lose their hypnotic glamour, but also I began to perceive a remarkable relationship between spiritual work and acting.

My acting studies began to flourish once again and before long I was asked to teach at a number of institutions in both the academic and therapeutic worlds. And as I progressed on this new path, I began to notice certain patterns and connections that gradually formed in me a fresh synthesis of the spiritual realm and the acting realm.

I, of course, am not alone. It is obvious to anyone in the performing arts that there is an active resurgence in spiritual matters. Famous actors and actresses are confessing their involvement in a wide variety of spiritual paths, ranging from lighthearted support of oriental healing methods to full-scale accounts of deep mystical revelations, trance channeling, and encounters with "the beyond."

In fact, virtually all my "almost famous" friends in the business are involved in some sort of spiritual quest. Some are into "isms" of all kinds, while others prefer work more aligned with therapy. Many have returned to the traditions of their family faiths with renewed vigor, insight, and commitment.

What sometimes happens, however, and this is the real tragedy, is this: highly dedicated seekers reach a certain point in their development where they feel compelled either to leave the performing arts and devote themselves totally to a spiritual tradition, or to drop their spiritual obligations and return to their beloved profession. Usually the person can do neither one and suffers unmercifully, sitting between two worlds.

This inertia can be harmful in a number of ways—even fatal. The seeker feels paralyzed as he or she sorts through the contradictions and competing inner voices. This may give way to a kind of defeatism, delivering a critical blow to one's self-image and undermining chances for contributions in either sphere (J.D. Salinger lovingly explores this theme by the way, in his superb story, "Zooey").

Occasionally the actor's ego, the aspect normally used to bolster courage and charm, gets unduly inflated by the exposure to "secret" or "occult" information. This sometimes results in abuses of this knowledge which inevitably backfire, turning against the actor and deterring his progress in uncountable ways.

Or just the opposite, the ego, overwhelmed by wrong notions of providence or seduced by sentimentalism, can deflate so much that the actor no longer functions normally. He loses his passion and theatrical drive, resembling in many ways the love-sick Pierrot.

So what is the serious actor/seeker to do? How can a performer in today's world maintain progress in the craft of acting and still evolve spiritually? What exactly *is* spiritual evolution? How can actor-training be a part of spiritual growth?

I have written this book to answer those questions—and many others. I hope it will serve as a link between the various spiritual paths and the art of acting. I believe it may also serve to clarify aspects of the great labyrinth, helping to guide those who may be in danger of becoming "casualties" of the search.

My personal bias is toward the mystic religions of the Far and Middle East. This should be taken into account by the reader. Specifically, my training is in Sufism, Kabbalah, Taoism, and Buddhism. I have had exposure to other paths such as American Indian Shamanism, Transcendental Hinduism, Esoteric Christianity and others, but there my involvement was "outer circle."

It should be understood that I am still a student of the world. I am not an enlightened being with access to the holy of holies. I have simply been allowed the life experiences that have provided me a glimpse at the mandala connecting spiritual work and acting. That is why I so readily "share the stage" in the course of the book by including lots of quotations and references to other sources for the reader's comparison.

A book, of course, cannot replace action. It is through actively working in the spiritual discipline of your choice or through maintaining concentrated efforts in your acting that any of this will be of value. Knowing what to do in these two worlds and how to do it is of utmost importance. Within these pages may be some insights that can help in one world or another. And even more, serve as a bonding conduit between both worlds, providing a catalyst for your own future investigations.

May your efforts benefit us all.

THE GOLDEN BUDDHA CHANGING MASKS

E.J. Gold, *The Troubadour*, Pen & Ink,
11" x 15", Rives BFK, 1987.

CHAPTER ONE

THE ACTOR

Historically, actors in the West have lived their lives as lowly social outcasts. When, on occasion, they managed to win royal favor, they enjoyed privileges beyond their station, but that was rare. Indeed, for many years actors could not even be buried in standard Christian cemeteries. Of course, once women joined the ranks of "players" during the Restoration era, actors were not only considered lowly by the mainstream society, but licentious as well. Even as recently as this century, actors were shunned from certain restaurants and rooming houses. It was not uncommon to see signs which read, "We do not accept Theatricals!"

This disreputable image of actors was at times justified. The stage has often been a bastion for misfits and scandalous rogues. Nevertheless, throughout history, actors have been tolerated, patronized, and often celebrated for their craft. They helped to create diversion from the toils of daily living.

Historically, their lowly social status did not inhibit the growth of acting as an art form. In just a few hundred years, ragged bands of players became full-fledged companies. In America, they even managed to establish *Broadway* as the Mecca for most Western actors. In recent years, their influence in society has grown at a phenomenal rate.

In a speech which he recently presented to a group of aspiring theatre students, Robert Cohen, author of several popular acting texts and Chairman of the Theatre Department at University of California at Irvine, resubmitted the obvious, yet astonishing reality: in today's world, the actor is virtually everywhere. Due largely to the global growth of television and film, actors now enjoy a position of power and prestige never before imagined. They are admired, followed, courted, and even consulted on matters previously reserved for experts.

And why not? In some cases, because of their avid search for truth, their constant research, public appeal, and sheer enthusiasm for discovery, actors manage to get results where others have failed. Their continual exposure to the pressure of being "on" makes them prime candidates for high-profile, high-pressure jobs.

Ronald Reagan, for example, is not alone in the "actor-turned-politician" category—that of politician certainly being one of the highest-profile and highest-pressure jobs available today. And many more actors are involved in projects that reach far beyond the stage and screen. Jane Fonda, Gregory Peck, Shirley Temple Black, Clint Eastwood, Marlon Brando, Mary Tyler Moore, Elizabeth Taylor, and thousands of other known and unknown actors work for charities, for research, for peace, for education, or for any number of other human causes that affect people in ways more formative than simply providing cultural diversion.

We could debate at length the value of this phenomenon. The fact remains, however, that currently, all over the world, it's "boom time" for actors. And with that in mind, we might very well ask, "What exactly *is* an actor?"

A look at what actors do underscores the current reality that actors are a category of people in society who seem to cross over a multitude of boundaries. They do everything: they sell products, they write films, direct films, produce plays, start companies, race cars, establish scholarships, give each other awards, create links with other nations, take political stands, donate money to countless charities, lend their popular appeal to needy causes, and, of course, they wash dishes, wait on tables, write jokes, bartend, or anything else they can find during their arduous journey to the "established actor" status. Sometimes, when they are talented and lucky enough—they actually act.

But what is acting? When actors act, what is it they are doing? There are many ways to answer that question, but I tend to agree with Richard Schechner that, among other things, they are providing society with a primary aesthetic and ritualistic ingredient he calls *restored behavior.*

Restored behavior is behavior that is simultaneously symbolic and reflexive. Moreover, it is a depiction of the self, usually perceived as stationary and fixed, as really being a role or set of roles.[1] In short, actors give evidence of the ephemeral aspect of the personality, while reaffirming essential human unity.

Regardless of the culture or style of performance, the actor is always involved in some form of restoration of behavior. One actor acts to help tell a story, another for political motives, another to provide emotional release or even a religious experience; yet they all adopt modes of working—a given score or style—which in some way verify their role in producing and reproducing an event.

However, the question remains: What is the ideal result of artistry in acting? What, if anything, does acting create in the actor?

Jerzy Grotowski, the director and researcher, renowned for his work with the Polish Lab theatre, held fast to a vision of the holy actor, a being capable of extraordinary leaps both physically and spiritually. I believe he was justified in his quest.

Actors share much in common with aspiring students of spiritual traditions, sometimes called *chelas or sannyasins* meaning "seekers." To begin with, both are genuine workers. The city of New York, for instance, owes much of its financial tenacity to the large population of aspiring actors pouring their theatrical "work" energy into the myriad service jobs they maintain. They both are willing to undergo highly disciplined and rigorous training. They both must be able to endure criticism and repeated rejection. They must be capable of enormous sacrifice and generosity. They both engage in considerable self-reflection and concentration. And both of them are continually tested for their dedication, progress, and sincerity. Most of all, they pursue their work out of love—not sentimental love—but love of the work itself which doesn't deny ulterior motives in both worlds.

The critical difference for the actor is that the actor needs an audience. The spiritual seeker can rely on a teacher, a community, and his own private sense of progress. The actor, on the other hand, is linked to the public.

This difference, however, does not diminish the possibility of acting being a way to spiritual unfoldment. On the contrary, I have reason to believe that under certain conditions, it can even enhance the process.

Unlike the spiritual adept, whose sacrifices result in ultimately overcoming the fear of death, the actor, and I refer here to the modern actor, may sacrifice greatly with little to show for this effort. And in the end, death still looms as the enemy—unvanquished—and unknown. To cope, he must rely on what meager religious teachings were accidentally acquired and must certainly wonder when the end is near: "Have I wasted my life? Did I turn to religion in time to save my soul?"

In antiquity, the actor was openly linked to the spiritual paths. In Egypt, Greece, Persia, Sumer, and in virtually all shamanistic tribal religions, the actor's work was sacred and an unquestioned contribution to the elevation of the soul. As a potentiality, it remains so to this day; only the link has been occluded by a number of factors, not the least of which are misguided notions of what spiritual work actually is.

It is my view, therefore, that once cleared of misconceptions, the art of acting can, if consciously desired, provide the circumstances which lead to spiritual awakening in the actor. However, before I begin to untie some of the knots surrounding the subject, I feel it is important to survey briefly the history of acting and chart the spiritual thread running throughout. From this view we may begin to see the patterns of spiritual work in theatre and thereby discern methods of working today.

E.J. Gold, *Inquiring Mind*, Pen & Ink,
11" x 15", Rives BFK, 1987.

CHAPTER TWO

HISTORY

In the West, we mark the dawn of theatre by the early Greek celebrations (dithyrambs) and the later, more structured, play festivals. This is convenient because the Greek civilization was recent enough that we can patch together reliable historical data. In reality, however, theatre, at least in tribal form, existed long before the Greeks, indeed since the dawn of time.

What format the early theatre took and to what extent the actor was spiritually evolved remains a mystery. By observing modern, so-called "primitive" societies we can begin to piece together information that strongly suggests that the original actor was the highly valued dancing, singing, mask-bearing tribal shaman.[1]

A shaman is a kind of priest who through special training and aptitude becomes the liaison between the mysterious, invisible non-ordinary realms, and the visible ordinary ones. The shaman must master a wide spectrum of talents including the all-important ability to induce self-propelled states of ecstasy or trance.[2]

His ability to voyage during trance states to other dimensions provides the shaman with very special knowledge. And because of this, he is considered by his immediate culture to have the ability to die and return to life many times during the course of his biological lifetime.[3] In this way, he is also the original mystic.

Unless you have had direct contact with a shaman, forget what you think you know. Many outside his culture, particularly in North America, have managed to dismiss the shaman as a Hollywood-style witchdoctor, branding him as a charlatan. This perception, however, is very far from the truth.

Real shamans are characterized by an elusive personality, a strong personal presence, and a strange clown-like irreverence for ordinary life. They are unpredictable in all things, yet have an uncanny and exact knowledge of their craft. For some, their powers are used exclusively to heal. Others are concerned with teaching or providing spiritual guidance.

In many ways the shaman resembles the Hindu Yogi with his paranormal abilities, deep trance/ meditation states, and religious authority. Yet, he differs from the classic Yogi model in that he is not turned exclusively inward, seeking enlightenment.

Instead, his knowledge is outwardly oriented, directed at serving the community.[4]

The world of the shaman is a world of "crazy wisdom" where consensus reality is sacrificed for the more potent non-consensus reality. As a result, en route to becoming a shaman, there are occasional bouts with what could be considered schizophrenic behavior. The shaman is trained not to become "reactive" during such episodes, which might cause premature redirection of his attention to the external world. Instead, he relies on an impartial attitude to the unfolding visions.

This eventually brings about a positive reintegration of his psyche. In this perspective, the shaman is the healed madman.[5]

Both shaman and non-reductionist analyst recognize and come to know the ultimate undifferentiated mystic reality, risking madness, in order to effect sanity in service to the community. In relation to this, Levi-Strauss says:

> The shaman plays the same dual role as a psychoanalyst...Actually the shamanic cure seems to be the exact counterpart to the psycho-analytic cure, but with an inversion of all elements...the psychoanalyst listens, whereas the shaman speaks.[6]

Whether for healing or other purposes, shamanic invocations of spirits and trance states were, and still are, often achieved through the use of masks and dance. Masks as representatives of spirits can transport the shaman to the psychic level needed to complete his task. Dance too serves to induce trance, as do drum rhythms, chanting, and psychotropic plants.

Unlike the shaman, the modern actor—especially in America—rarely uses masks per se although make-up and the creation of a public persona could be considered a mask. They nonetheless use other means to invoke characters as they play "storyteller", acting out our contemporary myths and fantasies on film, television, and the stage.

Shamans not only provide sacred functions involving the invisible realms of healing, soul navigation, dream interpretation, and so on, but they are also responsible for maintaining the tribal myths and legends through public storytelling performances.[7] So on the one hand we have a very serious and dedicated interior voyager and on the other, a crazy, visionary, schizzed-out storyteller. Is this not beginning to sound more and more like the actor we all know and love today?

An even clearer representation of the shamanic roots of acting can be seen in Japanese theatre. In Japan, the myths and legends are kept alive through the traditional forms of theatre, particularly the *Noh* theatre. In it, the actor is a purified, sanctified priestlike figure, subject to strict obligations.[8]

In addition, their belief system considers that gods are capable of inhabiting sacred objects as well as the body and character of an actor.[9] In Noh theatre, the mask and the actor both are considered sacred.

When the Noh actor sits and contemplates his mask before a performance, he is carrying out an ecstatic ritual that will allow the god that inhabits the mask to take full possession of him. This is in essence a shamanic technique. Shamans often use masks or objects to invoke higher or lower energies for the purpose of healing or inducing prophetic visions.

Through repeated sittings and experiences with the mask, the Noh actor opens to the invisible world. Through repeated sittings and experiences with objects, masks, rhythmic drumming, or chanting, the shaman opens to the invisible world. These repetitions are a formula of sorts, carrying both the actor and the shaman to other dimensions. For example, when the Noh actor climbs a tree on stage, in order to ascend to the sky, he, like the shaman, *actually experiences the ascent to heavenly spheres.*[10]

The major common denominator seems to be the element of repetition. Through repetition of sounds, movements, and any variety of incantations, both actor and shaman enter the trance state, giving them access to deeper experiences. I think it's interesting to note that rehearsal is a form of repetition; in fact, the French word for it is *repetition.*

Chances are, this strange singing and dancing wise/fool character organized rituals, repetitions, that were designed both to inform the tribe of his latest insight and to aid at times in creating another trance inducement.

This actor/shaman gradually evolved and refined over the years to become the actor celebrated in the early Greek dithyrambic rituals. However, this refining process split the shaman-role into two aspects: public and private.

Greece was famous for its oracles, which were connected to temples of the various Gods. Many of the warring Kings would send their messengers to the oracle of their patron god in hopes of getting advance probabilities and possible outcomes of particular campaigns.[11]

This "oracular magic" was in many ways a form of theatre using basic trance techniques and simulation-magic to arrive at a suitable "reading." The temple shamans would invoke the spirits of the two armies and then improvise a mock battle. They would then arrive at their conclusions based upon the improvisation.

The oracles were used by many people, not just kings. They provided information to help steer the lives of anyone who came to them. Getting to them, however, was not an easy task. It took special courage and fortitude to make the journey.

For example, the messengers or "audience" would undergo a rigorous preparation before seeing the oracle at Delphi. They would fast for three days, walk uphill several miles along a narrow path, all the while concentrating on their questions, until they reached a steambath outpost at the base of the mountain. After a purifying bath, they would walk at night, carrying a single torch, uphill along marble steps which led eventually to a tiny chamber, wherein they would encounter the priest who had also been prepared for the event.

Oracular ritual, then, at least at Delphi, seems to be closely aligned with private shamanic practices, similar to the ones described in the Carlos Castaneda books. The public events, like the mask, music, and dance rituals, were much more socially theatrical, occurring during celestial holidays and specific festivals honoring the gods. Both forms survived to fulfill a necessary function in the various levels of ritual participation.

Motivated by desires to appease the gods, public celebrations were used to create a mass healing event. This was accomplished by inducing the emotional state known as *catharsis*.

It is a well-known phenomenon that group energy can powerfully influence individual will. Sports arenas, funeral homes, and even comedy clubs all have their share of group consciousness. It is no secret that people can be easily swept into the pervading emotional tide of a crowd. The early Greeks capitalized on this phenomenon by provoking specific emotional reactions aimed at creating a healing unity among the audience. Catharsis was reached to purge them of their pain and restore health and happiness to the society.

This kind of "public privacy" shared by an audience is still enjoyed today, although to a greatly diminished degree. In fact, the diminishing of catharsis seems to have begun as early as the advent of competitive Greek play festivals. No longer were the plays communal rituals—they became a "work" to be enjoyed only through the barrier of competitive discernment.[12]

Related to this, I find that one event, above all others, intrigues me in the history of Greek theatre. It is generally understood that the theatre grew out of the religious music and dance that had for centuries been developed and passed along from generation to generation. It is also generally acknowledged that Thespis was the first to step from the chorus and create dialogue—thereby becoming the first individual actor, hence all actors are known as Thespians. But that event, which is given so little attention in most theatre history texts, strikes me as *the most* fundamental event in the history of acting.

Here we have a story of a man, a single human being, who forever changed the shape of theatre in the Western world. Yet, we know little or nothing about what actually happened. What occurred back then that allowed for such a change, especially considering the relatively stable progression of the dithyrambic festivals for so many years?

Well, knowing what I now know, and considering the perspective of this book, I am going to throw my hat in the ring and offer a possible, albeit presumptuous, speculation. It is my belief that Thespis did not just decide one day to invent dialogue. Nor did a group of his peers or any one maestro coerce him into such a fundamentally revolutionary act. It is my belief that he *transcended* the chorus; that through accident or device, he refined his nervous system to the degree that he was guided to step from the chorus—much like a shaman in trance or a contemporary channel. And he did this through no other means than those available to him in his art.

Am I suggesting that the father of western acting was a psychic channel? In a word, yes. And I further suggest that his channeling capabilities were developed through his function as an actor with the chorus.

Keep in mind that channeling is by no means a recent event. In fact, the Greek philosopher Socrates attributed much of his knowledge to the "voices" who counselled him regularly.[13] Also, channeling can take many forms. Nearly all composers, poets, artists, writers, inventors, and the like confess to feeling guidance of some kind or another. Certain people, however, become the embodied vocal conduit for direct contact with the beyond—a mouthpiece of sorts.

These "trance channelers" are capable of suspending their personal identities in order to allow other ones to take voice. They are more controversial from time to time, because of the disorienting theatrical effect of transmitting direct signals from the spirit world. But the fact is, all of us, and especially actors, are receivers of one kind or another. There are countless tales of performers reaching extraordinary heights during a performance, even during improvised performances, and then later feeling amazed and a bit humbled; feeling as though the performance came *through* them, not *from* them.

In actuality, we all experience glimpses of channeling every day. It comes as a "hunch," or hearing a song on the radio that seems to speak directly to you, or secret beliefs in lucky charms, self-coaching before a stressful event, message-filled dreams, getting a sudden urge to call a friend, and so forth.

One might argue that these are just the activities of the subconscious mind at work. Well, that unfortunate word — subconscious — should not be relegated to a lower order simply because of the prefix, "sub." That part of our consciousness is vast primal territory, just beginning to be explored by science. And anyway, why should a primal or preconscious state of awareness preclude highly sensitive receiving and transmitting powers?

Ordinarily, we habitually ignore the more subtle activities of our awareness in favor of the "real" world. Not so the artist and certainly not so the actor. An actor begins early on to observe every nuance of self in an effort to bring it more into the sphere of conscious direction. The effort to achieve this is the same effort and mechanism employed by psychics.

It seems evident to me that prophets, holy men, sages, alchemists, shamans, inventors, and even some scientists know what the Vedas have said all along: that *all knowledge is structured in consciousness.* Mastering the structure and accessing the variety of frequencies in the band of human consciousness is the work of all artists. Actors too, share this adventure, and have done so all along.

Sadly, the majority of humans on earth find the notion of other dimensions, voices, and higher consciousness either above or beneath their concerns. They content themselves with purely material pursuits.

That would be fine if that was all they did. Too often, however, these people have compulsive reactions against anyone whose ambitions run deeper than the accumulation of earthly power. Typically this manifests as fear which soon translates into anger, defense, and aggression.

Therefore, throughout history, those people wanting to reach their highest potential and avoid distraction in the form of persecution, joined together in groups, forming schools and brotherhoods. Most Christian monasteries and nunneries were established for similar reasons.

Schools in one form or another have flourished nearly everywhere in the world—in Egypt, in the highlands of Tibet, in the Caucasian mountains of Georgia, in the caves of Greece, and in the deserts of Persia, to name a few locales. Anyone who saw Peter Brook's film or read the book *Meetings With Remarkable Men* by G.I. Gurdjieff, has a fairly good idea of what is considered a school.

At these schools, then as now, certain laws were revealed and tested. These laws, which usually established experiential connections with mathematical law, natural order, and human possibility, were carefully guarded. In the Pythagorean schools, for example, novices had to undergo a five-year vow of silence before entering the serious phases of study.[14]

During specific intervals, however, the schools would reveal to the outside world portions of their discoveries. Pythagoras, for example, is credited with a number of major gifts to mankind including the invention of the Western musical scale, the laws governing certain geometrical shapes, as well as theories about the movements of the planets and stars and the transmigration of souls.[15]

When these discoveries were made public, it had to be done carefully. In many cases they shattered old concepts and radically changed man's existence. Therefore, like people carrying bright lights, the schools were careful not to shine them all at once, for fear of blinding or confusing those people accustomed to the dark.

Perhaps the Thespis event was one such revelation. Or perhaps it was a sudden and unplanned psychic phenomenon. Maybe it was a lucky "accident" that seemed to work, so they kept it.

Or maybe not. Maybe Thespis is a legend, a story created to explain the existence of dramatic structure. Perhaps the existing mystery schools never had contact with the theatre, and the plays enacted there had no relationship with the schools whatsoever. Yet, considering the priest-like role of actors at the time and the daring concepts exposed in Greek drama, I am inclined to believe that the mystery schools were at least partially involved in the work of the stage.

With the domination of the Roman Empire, theatre was forced to serve the popular demands of the day, quickly devolving into promotional extravaganzas which provided action, thrills, and elaborate spectacle. Greece too had its share of what Peter Brook calls the "rough theatre,"[16] but it was always balanced with a holy tradition. Roman rule, however, destroyed all that. What happened to the mystery schools and the impulse toward holy theatre?

They went underground as much true art does in occupied lands. As the empire began to crumble, and as the new Christian force began to take hold, actors were either absorbed into the rituals of the church, or forced to band together in small gypsy-like troupes.

The travelling troupes had the advantage of contact with people and ideas from other lands. It's conceivable that they could have formed links with other mystery schools from Byzantium or the Far East.

But any knowledge outside the sanctions of the ever more powerful church was considered heresy and was surely a dangerous preoccupation at the time. Therefore, certain laws and discoveries had to be hidden or "occluded" to insure protection against the church. It is even possible that the lamps of cosmic law and the knowledge of man's spiritual destiny were kept safe by being coded into the acrobatic and juggling shows of the time. (I know for a fact that not a few contemporary shows of a similar type are outgrowths of mystery school activities.)

These gypsies continued to develop their secret wisdom of herbs, divination, and fertility, while maintaining their living through magic shows, minstrel parades, and comic playlets. These characters are generally known to historians as *jongleurs*.

The popular Italian *jongleurs* maintained a family tradition of theatre and stayed together for generations, entertaining throughout Italy and abroad. Among other things, they presented clever scenarios using a collection of recurring stock characters (not unlike the American live comedy shows). The style came to be known as Commedia Del 'Arte and it showcased the characters of *Arrlechino, Puchinello, Dottore, Pedrolino, Colombina,* and so on. The fact that these characters were such strong archetypes suggests that some Italian players had access to the mystery school *law of human typicalities.*

This law is basic to nearly all mystic traditions with slight variances from culture to culture. Quite simply it is based on the premise that humans are all formed from a prescribed set of types with each type having a specific energy composition and life function. Some contemporary schools rely on the astrological model for this, others on the psychological post-Jungian models. I have found the best beginning model of the law of typicalities to be in Don Richard Riso's book, *Personality Types—Using the Enneagram for Self-Discovery.*

The Russian counterparts to the Italian players, known as *skomorokhi* (minstrels), also lived under the domination of the church. They had previously been priests who presided over many cyclic festivals and used their magical powers to heal, divine future events, and maintain ritual songs and incantations.[17] Under Christian rule, however, their works were limited to theatrical amusements including improvised comic dialogues, puppetry, and the famous dancing bear acts.[18]

I have no doubt that the reason the actors/priests in countries under Church rule were disempowered and shunned by the Christian leaders was not just because they worshipped "pagan" gods. I have a hunch they could put on a pretty hilarious and irreverent Saturday Night Satire, mocking the pomposities of the local clergy. And since reverence was mandatory and necessary for the installation of the new order, it was "hit the road" time for the minstrels.

Theatre, like nearly everything else, suffered the chaos of the Dark Ages. In the 10th century, however, it emerged in an organized form as brief biblical plays. These liturgical works were allegories enacted by the various craftsmen belonging to one of the many guilds. They were given permission and support by the Church to meet the communal need for the ritual of theatre.

The rituals, which proved to be a useful teaching tool for the Church, grew steadily in popularity. They soon became large festivals designed to help celebrate holy days such as Easter. These progressed into full scale pageant plays with multiple settings and a wide number of theatrical effects.

Within the confines of the Church, many of the essential elements of theatre were still at work in full force: the ritual of mass, the acoustical ambiance of a cathedral, focus-directing architecture, flickering red candles with a splash of color from stained glass windows on a marble floor, not to mention the chanting of nuns and monks, combining to create a holy spectacle that rivalled the mosques and temples of Persia.

And the mystery schools? In most of Europe, non-Christian mystery schools went underground, living in fear of the Catholic armies. Many of them enacted false conversions or retreated to obscurity in the south of France. Christian mystery schools, on the other hand, in the shape of monastic orders, flourished. And things stayed pretty much the same for generations until the Renaissance.

Formal theatre, which had blended symbiotically with the Church, asserted its independence. It moved swiftly through Tudor drama, improving all the while, until it managed to reach its finest moment during the Elizabethan period with the unquestionable genius of William Shakespeare.

Shakespeare's work still looms as the outstanding example of theatre that is elevated, yet honest and true. His plays manage to cross nearly all barriers of time and space, fulfilling a metaphysical aim of keeping company with the Absolute, if only briefly, before coming back down to earth.[19] In fact, his plays are so numerous, the language so full, the plots so different, that many scholars have entertained the notion that they were not written by him at all. They contend that because of the lowly status awarded a playwright at the time, other poets actually wrote the plays, but conspired to pin the credit on an actor named William.

The "conspiracy" theory remains unresolved due to the fact that British authorities refuse to exhume Shakespeare (a fact supporters of the conspiracy theory see as evidence in their behalf). Regardless of who wrote them, the fact is they exist and actors have performed them for centuries.

The plays are full of mystical elements which reflect the free thinking of the day. *Hamlet, Midsummer Night's Dream, The Tempest, King Lear, Macbeth* and many others approach subjects considered heretical in the not-too-distant past. The Ghost of Hamlet's father visiting him, for example, or the Druidic and magical playfulness of Oberon and Titania's woodland world, the conjuring witches in *Macbeth*, the recurring references to astrological fatalism in *Romeo and Juliet, Cymbelene*, and so on, all display the new freedoms enjoyed by the theatre of the day.

Yet, at the same time, there arose a strong reaction against such freedom. The reaction took the shape of religious persecution against the Neo-platonist movement and anyone delving into the mystical arts without strict sanctions from the Church. In 1600, the outspoken Hermetic philosopher Giordano Bruno, for example, was burned for his interests in Egyptianism and magic, as a symbolic warning to others.[20]

Not surprisingly, under such heated conditions, many of the free thinkers of the day retreated to the relative sanctuary of secret societies. These were newly adopted mystery schools with links to the ancient lineages.

John Dee, the popular scientist, poet, and one of the most celebrated men of the Elizabethan age, came under attack for his interests in "occult" philosophies. One such attack came in dramatic form when Christopher Marlowe presented his play *Doctor Faustus*. The play presented a rather seedy portrait of a conjurer who sells his soul to Lucifer, but repents unsuccessfully at the hour of his death. The play was an obvious attempt to disgrace Dee by insinuating that he and others like him were malevolently conjuring devils.[21]

Shakespeare, who wrote of witches, faeries, and demons, must have come under careful scrutiny at the time as well. Perhaps it was due to his popularity—or to the fact that actors were considered damned anyway—that he never endured the kind of public defamation John Dee had to withstand. Of course, Shakespeare merely wrote about such things, he never openly admitted to delving into them as John Dee had done.

However, during the latter period of his writing, Shakespeare created *The Tempest*. In it, Prospero, the main character, is a conjurer—but his magic is white magic, used for utopian ends. This play did much to cool the current witch-hunt frenzy and establish white Cabala as legitimate. And in many ways it helped to vindicate John Dee, who had fallen from a position of prominence to obscurity and poverty.[22]

As the Restoration era settled in and the theatre of manners took over, the spiritual dimension of acting waned considerably. It was to resurface with a vengeance in the work of Ibsen, Strindberg, Yeats, Artaud, and many others involved in the realist, symbolist and surrealist movements of the late 19th and early 20th centuries.[23]

These movements gave rise to the next wave of playwrights and men of the theatre whose work resonates and informs nearly all of contemporary drama. Chief among them are Ionesco, Meyerhold, Beckett, Grotowski, and Stanislavski.

Ionesco penetrated into our collective reactions to light and shadow. He also forced us to hear our own mad laughter as we come face to face with the modern cycle of acceleration, proliferation, and destruction. Meyerhold attempted to demystify acting by creating a new set of training tools called *biomechanics*. With it, he introduced the notion of the actor's body as an athletic, ultimately acrobatic instrument, capable of responding to theatrical situations with total non-linear commitment. Beckett gave us the power of his singular gift for the theatrical metaphor. His *Waiting for Godot* will most probably live on as the greatest dramatic masterpiece of this century. Grotowski shed all previous notions of acting and began a true laboratory of investigation where the soul of the actor took precedence over any other element.

It is Stanislavski's work, however, that I find to be the most profoundly influential for the Western actor, particularly in terms of spiritual advancement. This might seem odd at first, especially considering the extent to which his work has been associated with dry, typically non-spiritual naturalism. But the more I delved, the more I realized that he had been using, consciously or unconsciously, some important mystery school ideas. These ideas were, and still are, powerful tools used in spiritual training. Some of the techniques I shall describe in later chapters.

That brings us, with no claim of exhaustive analysis, to the contemporary scene. Actors today are working in all media and in all countries. The explosion is fantastic. And in the West, particularly in the United States, actors are still being trained with numerous variations on Stanislavski's original work. With only a slight shift in emphasis and approach, spiritual work could be included in this acting training.

What do I mean by *spiritual* work? Well, virtually all religious sources suggest that we are here to prepare for a form of graduation. Each religion has its own curriculum, so to speak, with a hierarchy of development, suggesting grades or levels. Most world religions adhere to the notion of reincarnation, cycles of return visits until we are beyond the need of the human experience. Christianity and certain other religions adhere to the one-shot idea: you make it this time or not at all. Regardless of the belief system, they all function within the same model: *steps moving to an ultimate goal.*

Each religion has its own unique yardstick to measure progress along the way. Most often this is the appraisal by an elder or a group of peers who are somewhere further up the ladder. What unites them is that as the new spiritual awareness takes root, the adepts usually speak of feeling closer to God; they take more responsibility for their actions and exhibit remarkable personal fortitude, fearlessness, compassion, purposefulness, and striking individuality.

In my opinion, the aim of all spiritual work boils down to two basic results. One group wishes to graduate from earth for good, make it to a higher plane such as Heaven or Nirvana or wherever. There they hope to live for eternity in "God's place." The other group hopes to learn the ropes so well, they can consciously return to this plane of existence and help others, thereby enhancing everyone's chances for liberation. Some in this latter category assume the added responsibility of awakening the creator who, by the misuse of man's free will, has fallen asleep into his own creation.[24]

Pretty heady stuff. And not normally the province of the theatre. In today's world, an actor's aim is usually more aligned with worldly pursuits. "Making it" is the paramount concern. I am compelled to ask, "What is the purpose of making it?"

Keep in mind, the spiritual dimension of acting is not for everyone. It is only for those few souls who hunger for a deeper calling, who need to serve a purpose higher than their personal concerns. We are conditioned to see that kind of sacred life-aim as outside the art of theatre. That perception, however, is rapidly changing.

It is apparent to me that throughout history there has been a thread of spiritual influence weaving itself into the art of acting. We must recognize this and assume responsibility for nurturing its growth. And given the vast influence of actors in the world today, it strikes me as a critical time to return to a sanctified approach to the art. Herein are some tools, reminders, and ideas that can guide the actor who is so inclined towards such an aim.

And as a teacher of mine once said, "Nobody knows it all." I do not claim to have all the answers. However, I am certain that this book can help provide a strong, practical foundation for anyone willing to begin what must be done.

E.J. Gold, *Mystic Realist*, Pen & Ink,
11" x 15", Rives BFK, 1986.

CHAPTER THREE

STANISLAVSKI, THE MYSTIC REALIST

In his autobiography, *My Life in Art,* Constantin Stanislavski gives us a candid look at his family life in Moscow and the events which formed his interest in theatre. By all accounts, he was a normal young boy, a bit privileged perhaps—not all families can afford to build a small stage for their kids to play on— but normal nonetheless. What thrilled him the most was being allowed to go with his father to see the opera.

After witnessing a number of performances which moved him deeply, he began to strongly focus his energy towards his new-found desire—to be an actor. His father, thinking it was a passing phase, gave him free reign to entertain his fantasies, at least until he was of age. At that time he was expected to join the family business.

However, Constantin had other plans. He felt compelled to try his hand at acting. Knowing he would displease his father and not wanting his family to risk public ridicule in case he failed, Constantin changed his name from Alexiev, his real name, to Stanislavski, a stage name. Nevertheless, his father soon found out about it. But it was too late, Constantin was hooked.

Luckily for Stanislavski, who at first was not a very good actor, wealth and life-circumstances allowed him the luxury of dabbling in the theatre long enough to establish himself as a fairly competent actor. Later in life he was considered a masterful actor, admired by all who saw him perform.

What is remarkable is that he went beyond that. For some reason, he felt compelled to uncover the underlying conditions which led to artistic inspiration. During his search, he quickly realized that there was no reliable process of training the actor. No one seemed to have a clear idea of how an inspired moment occurred and why it was so fleeting. Everything was left, more or less, to chance. He could not tolerate this unnecessary condition and devoted his life to the consistent investigation of what a person can do to be a truly great actor.

He gave himself to the quest of discovering the laws governing inspiration. He was trying to understand the invisible forces that move an actor's soul. Somehow, either through accident or design, he came upon ideas that are in alignment with mystery school practices. And as a result of his efforts, actors now have reliable methods of preparing themselves for the stage.

For example, one of the basic and most pervasive beginning training tools in nearly all spiritual disciplines is activating comprehensive self-observation. In fact, the Russian mystic Gurdjieff used this technique almost exclusively as he labored to endow people with the power of self-remembering:

Knowledge of oneself is a very big, but a very vague and distant, aim... Self-study is the work or the way which leads to self-knowledge. But in order to study oneself one must first learn *how to study*, where to begin, what methods to use...The chief method of self-study is self-observation. Without properly applied self-observation a man will never understand the connection and the correlation between the various functions of his machine [body], will never understand how and why on each separate occasion everything in him 'happens.'[1]

Compare that with what Stanislavski states:

If you only knew how important is the process of self-study! It should continue ceaselessly, without the actor even being aware of it, and it should test every step he takes.[2]

Nearly all acting approaches give at least some attention to powers of observation and self-study. This is because, quite obviously, the actor must know his own manifestations before attempting to harness them for theatrical use.

The prerequisite for advanced powers of observation is concentration. Highly developed powers of concentration can be seen in many endeavors, from martial arts to the prayers of a Trappist monk. Of course certain activities utilize different aspects of this power. A race car driver must have a particularly sharp form of concentration while driving at speeds in excess of 200 mph. The sculptor, on the other hand, must demonstrate a longer span of concentration of a quality exactly suited to the material he is shaping.

A number of religious disciplines are notable for their unusual dedication to the power of concentration. Zen Buddhism, for example, is famous for its rigorous concentration, especially as it applies to meditation. And there is a Sufi technique designed to expand or contract the field of awareness by diffusing the vision and not following any particular thing, even in a busy marketplace. Hindu and Tibetan monks will often spend long hours concentrating on a painting or a candle flame. Catholics pray the rosary and Quakers sit in peaceful silence.

And actors? Here is what Stanislavski says about *concentration* as it relates to the work of the actor:

>...If you gave a man a magic mirror in which he could see his thoughts, he would realize that he was walking about on a heap of broken pieces of his begun, unfinished and abandoned thoughts. Just like a shipwrecked vessel. Pieces of torn velvet material, bits of broken masts....and every sort of flotsam and jetsam.
>
>This is what thoughts of a beginner in the studio, who can neither concentrate his attention, nor keep it fixed on one object, are like.
>
>And so we have come to the first step of the creative art of the stage, a step that is unalterable and common to all—concentration of attention, or to put it more briefly, concentration.[3]

And:

...In mastering it and in learning to concentrate all the powers of your organism on some particular part of it, you learn at the same time the art of transforming your thought into, as it were, a fiery ball. Your thought, strengthened by your attention and put into words, in a definite rhythm will, provided it is spoken by you in a state of full concentration, break through all the conventional stage situations you may have to deal with, and find its way straight to the heart of the spectator.[4]

Stanislavski introduced the use of circles of concentration to train his actors. In this technique, the actor expands his or her concentration in an ever widening circle, as far as can be sustained; when the circle begins to waver it must withdraw to a smaller radius which can be easily sustained by visual attention. Gifted actors can maintain several circles at once—monitoring the stage picture and the attention of the audience while sustaining laser sharp focus in a specific unit of action.

Stage presence, that magnetic quality in some actors, seems to be a by-product of a powerfully expanded circle of concentration. In my experience, it is the result of expanding a circle to include the entire audience, while simultaneously maintaining very focussed and detailed onstage circles.

Obviously film actors must utilize their circles of concentration differently. To insure that their subtle camera reality is small enough, yet potent enough to captivate the viewer, they must hold a tight circle that is just wide enough to include the camera. And of course, all good actors instinctively manipulate their focus of attention with clarity and discrimination.

Once concentration is established and self-observation begins to occur, actors, like adepts, must
next begin to understand the division of functions in
the instrument. They notice that the body has a
moving function (dance, mime, postural alignment,
etc.), a thinking function (learning lines, script
analysis, research, etc.), a feeling function (sensitivity, emotional expression, sensuality, pain, etc.)
and finally an instinctive function (reflex reactions,
hunger, gut-level impressions).[5]

Every actor has a different chemistry and was
born with an instrument that is composed of a certain configuration of the aforementioned functions.
This means that each person will have a different
reaction to the same stimulus; he or she will process
it differently. How they process it is governed in part
by the *type* of person they are. Some actors are the
shy type offstage but gangbusters onstage or vice
versa. Some are intellectually motivated and must
build their character's mindset while others might be
emotionally oriented and would first choose to explore the emotional dimension of a character.

When actors begin to understand what type of
people they are and how they are uniquely conditioned to perceive the world, they can then begin to
reprogram their instruments, taking them into territories outside their types.

In advanced work, the actor/adept can
reprogram the instrument for a specific aim. An
actor, for example, may wish to create a character
which is radically different from his personal configuration. The spiritual adept may wish to overcome habitual mind patterns and simply open his

heart to God. The initial step, before any of this happens for actors and adepts alike, is to arrive at an impartial, or neutral, state of being.

It is from this relative neutrality that they begin to perceive a possibility of deeper, more objective neutrality from which they can range very far with no fear of losing themselves.

In India, the system most employed for this purpose is the balancing of the chakras. Chakras are seven basic energy centers that correspond to certain glands in the body. There is a lot of research and written material concerning the chakras, so it is not necessary to go into detail here. I will, however, give the location of the centers and their corresponding glands.

The first chakra is located at the base of the spine and corresponds to the adrenals, the second is located in the center of the pubic bone and relates to the sexual glands, the third is located at the navel and relates to the spleen, the fourth is located just below the sternum at the solar plexus and relates to the thymus, the fifth is located at the throat in the nook where the clavicle bones meet and it relates to the thyroid, the sixth is located in the lower forehead between the eyebrows and corresponds to the pituitary gland, and the seventh and final chakra is located at the center of the top of the head, corresponding to the pineal gland.

When these various glands are balanced, a person can enjoy a steady, blissful neutrality. When the chakras are out of balance (the norm for most people), there exist cravings, disorders, and perceptual anomalies.

The chakra system processes vital energy from the air called "prana" and uses it to stimulate the various centers, achieving a variety of results—one of which is this elusive neutral state. Regarding the chakra system, Stanislavski states:

> I have read what the Hindu say on this subject. They believe in the existence of a kind of vital energy called Prana, which gives life to our body. According to their calculation, the radiating center of this Prana is the solar plexus. Consequently, in addition to our brain which is generally accepted as the nerve center and psychic center of our being, we have a similar source near the heart, in the solar plexus...[6]

Now, of course, the Indian system is much more exact than what Stanislavski describes (he mentions only the *Manipura* chakra at the solar plexus, which the Hindus view as the *will center*—the spiritual vortex of free will), but he does give the fundamental basis for contacting the powerful energies needed for powerful acting. He further relates his personal use of the chakra idea in achieving a link between the mental and the emotional center, resulting in the ability to "commune with myself onstage either audibly or in silence, and in perfect self-possession."[7] While not exactly an expert in spiritual disciplines, his motives were clear: searching for means to secure excellence in acting.

Yet, how wonderful to know that he came to formulate his own experiments by borrowing at times from the spiritual techniques of the Hindus. It's even more wonderful when one realizes that modern actors, especially in the 1960's, in an attempt to be avant-garde and break new ground, adopted elements of Hindu spiritual disciplines. Stanislavski had beaten them to it by several decades!

In addition to self-observation, concentration, and the use of chakras, Stanislavski also recognized physical tension as an enemy to artistic expression. Nearly everyone recognizes that excess tension reduces flexibility and vocal range. But the most destructive aspect of excess tension in acting, and in spiritual work, is the fact that tension hinders access to the subconscious.

That is why Yoga masters, Tai Chi teachers, and spiritual counselors of all kinds encourage relaxation. Relaxing the mind and body allows freer circulation, a calmer, more clear state of mind which in turn allows greater appreciation for the subtler fields of energy in the body. Sounding very much like a Chinese Tai Chi teacher, Stanislavski says:

> Madame Sonora has drawn your physical attention to the movement of energy along a network of muscles. This same kind of attention should be fixed on ferreting out points of pressure in the process of relaxing our muscles—a subject we have already considered in detail. What is muscular pressure or spasm except moving energy that is blocked?
>
> From your experiences last year in the sending out of certain rays or wordless communications, you know that energy operates not only inside us but outside as well; it wells up from the depths of our beings and is directed to an object outside ourselves.
>
> ...It is important that your attention move in constant company with the current of energy, because this helps to create an endless, unbroken line which is so essential to our art.[8]

And:

...therefore, be quite bold in throwing off as much tension as you possibly can. You needn't think for a moment that you will have less tension than you need. No matter how much you reduce tension, it will never be enough...Your own physical and spiritual truth will tell you what is right. You will sense what is true and normal better, when you reach the state that we call, *I am.*[9]

The flow of energy and the active sending out of rays is the conscious utilization of the etheric body in man—our soul. In Taoist terms he is referring to the flow of "chi" in the body along the meridians which should flow unobstructed in a person preparing for high spiritual training.

Then, not only does he imply that courage is needed to, in his words, "throw off tension," but he clearly states that it will be rewarded with a particular state of awareness called "I am." This is amazing to me because this "I am" is the state of graceful presence referred to, in exactly the same way, by Buddhists, Hindus, Sufis, Kabbalists, Christians— virtually all religions.

A Kabbalist teacher and friend of mine told me not long ago that according to his tradition, the problem with humanity is the addition of an object. He explained that scripturally, I am is divine. But man felt compelled to include more, making phrases like these: I am angry, or I am an American, or I am a mechanic. As you see, division and confusion begins with the inclusion of one extra word.

It seems that spiritual work and acting techniques developed by Stanislavski intersect and share common elements that are working towards common goals. Both realms work to achieve powers of concentration, self-observation, impartiality, knowledge of the energy centers of the body, relaxation, presence, discernment of what is true, and a balanced state of dedication to something higher than oneself—be it God, the Absolute, Jesus, Art, or whatever name we give it.

And above all, it is amazing to know that the state of grace recognized by most religions as I am is also held by Stanislavski, the father of modern acting, as the ultimate goal for actors.

Much of what has been established in American acting owes its existence to this Russian, who for too many years has been dismissed as nothing more than the vanguard of realism. The Actor's Studio and other such offshoots did indeed refine and Americanize his concepts; but only enough to feed the increasing demand for cinematic reality. What of our deeper, spiritual realities?

It is time to re-evaluate the course of acting today, to reinvigorate the spiritual impulses behind Stanislavski's life work. He was a realist, yes, and concerned himself with the behavioral truth of acting. His quest, however, was far beyond achieving natural behavior in acting. Stanislavski was an actor, director, and researcher; but he was more the spiritual mystic than most people realize. Let us take his original question and work as he did to find an answer: what is it that brings inspiration into an actor?

E.J. Gold, *And Now for Something Entirely Different,*
Pen & Ink, 11" x 15", Rives BFK, 1987.

CHAPTER FOUR

THE TAO OF ACTING

There is a moment in the theatre when something very satisfying happens. The actor and audience merge in a way that defies description. We recognize it when it arrives. Everyone feels it. We know when it "clicks"; when the timing, the breath, the contact is so alive, it transcends ordinary reality and becomes something else, something extraordinary.

That magical moment manifests indirectly, in a way that is similar to how scientists observe atomic particles in a cloud chamber. They cannot actually see them, but they can observe their effects as they travel through the cloud molecules. In the chamber of the theatre, the effect is sometimes a burst of laughter, a warmth throughout the space, a gasp or even a stunned silence. These moments hint at something tasted, something deeply experienced outside the tyranny of words.

The ancient Chinese recognized this mystery as a quality inherent in nature. They knew, also, the importance of living in harmony with it. This unnamable quality came to be known as the *Tao,* which translates as "The Way." As they lived and worked in accordance with it, they realized that it was a wondrous dynamic consisting of an infinitely complex interplay of "male" and "female" energies. They discovered that the great dance between the female quality (Yin) and the male quality (Yang) is responsible for all aspects of manifest creation.

If we take this fundamental principle and apply it to acting, we see that in the theatre, the audience is in the dark, sitting in the passive mode which is Yin. The actors are in the light, in the active mode which is Yang. The outside of the theatre is Yang and the inside Yin. The empty stage is Yin and the seats are Yang until the audience which is composed of a particular combination of Yin and Yang energy sits, ready to receive—making the seats Yin and the stage Yang. Yin is soft, yielding, cool, and feminine. Yang is hard, unyielding, hot, and masculine. Stage movements are an orchestration of the two qualities that guide the focus of the audience and gradually unfold the spectacle.

The Chinese Yin/Yang symbol of the Tao gives us a clue to the more profound dynamics of the concept. In the Yang side there exists a portion of Yin and in the Yin, a portion of Yang. And so it is that every actor should have within him a portion of the audience and the audience should have within it a portion of the actor. When this relationship is fulfilled, there is a transcendence, a "lifting off" that everyone senses, but cannot speak of, because the act of even beginning to speak of it breaks the moment.

Actors have been told time and again, "acting is reacting," "follow your instincts," and the ever-popular "play the moment." These are all truisms that try to instill the importance of equilibrium in stagecraft. And as the Taoists know, too much of one quality will cause imbalance and decay. If an actor is all Yang, obsessively pushy, delivering without the Yin quality of listening, the performance will suffer. By the same token, if an actor is too passive, unable to take stage and deliver when necessary, the performance will, of course, suffer.

Each of us is a product of the union of male and female energies. Each of us has a particular mix of the two and every mix is different. Some men are composed of a lot of Yin energy and women sometimes have considerable Yang energy. And the composition is in constant flux depending upon myriad circumstances.

All good actors know, if not consciously then unconsciously, how to redistribute their personal composition of energy to suit a particular characterization. A man playing Hamlet, for example, might choose to demonstrate the character's transition from the passive Yin state, to the active Yang state, over the course of the whole show. It might occur gradually as Hamlet slowly begins to see how trapped he is by his excessive Yin qualities, the Ophelia and Gertrude within himself. He wrestles with his yielding weaknesses, which are repulsive to him, by lashing out at Gertrude and hiding mentally from Ophelia. Yet, when he finally manages to activate his Yang energy, to take action, it is too uncontrolled, too late, and ends in tragedy.

And more specifically, within the framework of a soliloquy, an actor could apply the same concepts. Certain passages could be appropriately chosen as internal and soft while other passages are hard and masculine. The Yin and Yang qualities of speech, movement, and breath could all be used to orchestrate the flow of words. This way of viewing acting, as you see, can become increasingly detailed, helping to shape every facet of a performance.

The important thing to remember with this concept of the Tao is not the difference between Yin and Yang, but the dynamic symbiosis of their relationship. One does not exist without the other; they need each other in order to function. And when all the elements are in order and the equilibrium of energies somehow line up, then there is that magical connection, harmony with the Tao.

There are countless stories of actors who, after a particularly spectacular performance, scratch their heads and marvel at the way everything seemed to flow. They take some credit for being prepared for excellence to occur, but most of them bow to the mystery, knowing deep inside that they have been merely part of an event, not the event itself. An echo of this is expressed by Taoist Master Ni Hua Ching:

> Neither does the sage act; it is the power of the Tao that acts through him whether he is overtly active or inactive. He simply becomes like a leaf

riding the wind of the Tao, unable to tell if he is carrying the wind along or the wind is carrying him. Any individual effort obstructs the flow of this infinite potency.[1]

It would be easy to assume that the path of the Tao is a kind of simple-minded "go with the flow" philosophy, but that is not the case. The precepts sound simple, but authentic simplicity is not easy to achieve. The Taoists recognized early that much of man's suffering was due to his own unconscious need for intellectual complexities. This urge to prove himself the most clever creature on earth resulted in an unfortunate habit of unconscious meddling. Certainly today with the advent of world pollution, animal extinction, and nuclear threat, we can see the results of that habit. The Taoist path avoids meddling and instead supports appreciation for what is called *the uncarved block*.

They believe that things in their original simplicity have a natural power and that meddling with that simplicity reduces the power, subjecting it to weaknesses.[2] "Go with your instincts" is a command given to actors to remind them of their own uncarved block, their pure primal power. Too much carving, too much clutter in a role will certainly weaken the effect.

To achieve true simplicity is to be conscious of the dynamic processes in life while participating in harmony with the natural order. One must know when to be active and when to be inactive. To master this moment-to-moment discernment takes a combination of experience and trust—sometimes called faith.

The ultimate act of faith in the Tao of theatre would be improvisation. It takes a lot of experience to be able to act effectively in an improv and even more faith. That is why audiences are so responsive to it. They take great delight in knowing the moment is being constructed *at the moment*, for their eyes only. Plus, the actors are forced to "play the moment" and indeed, when one is acting without a script, acting is definitely "reacting." This is always more exciting, more like a sporting event where the outcome isn't fixed. And when experienced performers take the improvisational leap of trust, the results can neither be matched nor repeated.

Of course, there isn't a moment that is not happening now. However, actors and audiences often prefer to hide behind the veneer of rehearsed moments. It seems safer to them that way, although in fact there is more danger of the performance going dead (not to mention the audience). Things that do not carry the power of immediacy tend to drift away from us, forcing us in turn to drift away. That is not what theatre is all about. All experienced actors know that awful feeling when the audience begins to drift. Suddenly, in those moments, the actor's work seems useless and banal.

That does not mean that a rehearsed performance cannot be completely alive. On the contrary, it can become a very enjoyable structured improvisation, the structure being the preparation before the opening. However, they are the best actors who know, truly know, that every moment onstage is an improv, regardless of how many shows have been performed. And they are the wisest actors who come to know that in life, every moment is an improv; there are no second takes.

Essentially then, the Tao of acting is to be simple, to act in accordance with the natural laws of Yin and Yang, to be spontaneous and true to the moment— while maintaining an energy flow appropriate to the overall equilibrium of the show. When this is accomplished, there is artistry, there is transcendence, there is the Tao of acting.

E.J. Gold, *Femme au Chapeau Chic avec Popcorn,*
Pen & Ink, 11" x 15", Rives BFK, 1987.

CHAPTER FIVE

WHAT IS GOING ON HERE?

Try this sometime: sit in a theatre or at a movie house and during the performance, pull your awareness from the show and ask yourself quietly, "What is going on here?" As you do this, look around you, at the faces of those who are watching and see if, in the deepest part of yourself, you don't feel a faint collective motive at work.

Essentially, it is a group of humans in voluntary captivity watching other humans being other humans (or creatures or dancers or whatever). Granted, there are issues weighed, manners displayed and critiqued, and emotions acted out within some vision or other. But content aside, what is the meaning behind the form? Why go to the theatre at all?

The standard answers are usually, "Because it's an escape"; "It supplies a necessary communal experience"; "It can force people to confront their weaknesses or their political inertia." True, it does all that. Perhaps not every time or always to the same degree of success, but generally we see it in terms of what we get from it.

That still does not answer my question. Those benefits are results, by-products of a process. What *is* the process? What goes on at the theatre?

Allow me to provide some food for thought. In order to do this I am going to have to borrow, albeit lightly, from the world of physics. Please bear with me, I hope to do this with clarity and simplicity, and only to the degree that it illuminates my point. In order to do this, I am going to rely on the writings of Itzhak Bentov, the bio-medical engineer and inventor whose books, *Stalking the Wild Pendulum* and *The Cosmic/Comic Book,* I highly recommend.

Now, scientists realize that all matter, at the subatomic level, is really a pattern of energy that moves and reacts according to known and sometimes unknown laws. Astonishingly, this energy acts not only as particles but also as waves (a condition that is still a mystery). These waves interact with other waves, and that interaction results in various phenomena.

Sound, for example, is a wave energy emitted from a resonating system. Our heart, as Bentov so eloquently points out, is in fact a resonating system. The brain we know also gives off waves, as do our bodies. In actuality, we as humans participate in a miraculous electromagnetic and thermodynamic event on this planet. And as a result, we actually do emit and receive vibratory energy.[1]

Now, waves interact and if they are too different, they will assume a beat frequency together, meaning there will be periodic moments where they cancel each other out. Sometimes, however, they can reach a kind of understanding and *rhythm entrainment* occurs. This means they give up their little differences in favor of a new frequency. This new frequency has the potential to be a coherent wave pattern—that means little to no modulation in the pattern—in other words, unified.[2]

Another aspect of vibration is the fact that if a certain frequency is activated, say, a note on a piano, other frequencies will respond in sympathy. Pluck middle C and the C strings of other octaves will vibrate, as will certain other notes in mathematical sympathy to the original.[3]

Consider the audience as a massive oscillating system, a veritable battery of energy. When they are led to focus their energy on, let's say, performer A, she is receiving a dose of vibratory energy outside the normal experience. If the performer has had training and preparation, she can charge her instrument with that energy and through skillful means transform it into a condensed and refined impression. She literally can strike a chord in herself, and the soul of the audience will respond in sympathetic vibration.

If the performer's instrument is damaged or unable to handle the sudden jolt of energy, she will most often close off the flow to protect herself or will become uncontrolled, wildly allowing the energy to distort her performance. This lack of finesse is sensed by the audience, of course, and governs their willingness to focus their attention. And if you lose the attention of an audience, well...the show fails. The quality of a performance, then, in the purest sense, is really judged on the vibratory level.

The battery of energy provided by an audience depends on a number of factors, not the least of which is expectation. Every audience comes into the theatre with certain expectations and that energy is the initial quality the actor faces. When a comedian is famous and generally accepted as funny, all he needs to do is walk onstage and the expectations give him a free ride at first. He must still fulfill or improve upon that initial energy, but the atmosphere was charged for him. A lesser-known comedian faces a low-expectation energy field and must overcome it each time—a task that can overwhelm even strong performers.

Using Bentov's vibratory model, during the course of a performance, when things are clicking, the variety of wave formations in the house and onstage have ceased the occasional cancelling (beat frequency), and everyone can enjoy frequent and sustained moments of rhythm entrainment. You've no doubt seen birds flying in remarkable synchronicity; that is another example of rhythm entrainment. The actors and audience are, in a way, flying together.

The experience of theatre then, could simply be for the pleasure of flying. I believe, however, that the pleasure, and even the flying, is a by-product of a process even more subtle and necessary.

The Russian mystic and teacher, G.I. Gurdjieff, introduced to his group of students a system of study which, among other things, outlines man's position in the hierarchy of cosmic energy. His system, although new to Western man, had been in use for many years in the Russian mystery schools. It was a version of the table of elements based on something called "the law of octaves," in other words waves, vibrations.

According to this system, as interpreted by P.D. Ouspensky, man's potential and sole hope of advancement is dependent upon the collection and absorption of substances Gurdjieff called "hydrogens." In this system, the basic substances for maintaining life are hydrogens H768, H192, and H384; food, air, and water. What was surprising to many of his students was also the inclusion of hydrogens 48, 24, and 12—representing *impressions* as a major source of life-sustaining substance.[4] In fact, Gurdjieff explained that impressions were the *most important* substance. For if denied them a person would perish even more quickly than if he were denied air.

If we consider carefully the implication of this, we can begin to see why people go to the theatre, or to movies, or to museums, and so on. They are literally being fed. Of course their ability to digest the impression thoroughly is a different matter, and a constant frustration to artists everywhere.

I have experienced, to some degree, what Gurdjieff was teaching. In times of very low energy, for example, I have been exposed to a powerful impression like a beautiful meteor shower, a concert, or standing in front of a Van Gogh, and I have felt refreshed afterward; lighter and more energetic. In fact, that may be the very law at work when someone goes on holiday for a "change of scenery."

In my view, part of what is going on at the theatre is this: a group of individual energy fields collect themselves in a contained space and through the help of some careful manipulation of mood, they relinquish their individual energy field by focusing their attention on the stage. Then, other humans, who have been trained to handle it, take on the additional charge—transmuting it into refined impressions which serve as food for the audience. Ideally it is good food which raises their vibratory level.

If their job is done well, the actors are rewarded with an accelerated vibrational wash (applause), plus the expanded consciousness their art affords them. Not to mention the satisfaction of knowing their work may be serving to upgrade the vibratory level of a set of fellow oscillators, improving the entire field for everyone!

This concept is a far cry from the image of a bunch of coarse actor misfits who want to parade their personalities in blatant self-promotion. Of course, it is an impractical perspective for unskilled performers who have not reached a level of objective awareness. Even for the advanced actor, this is only a hint at the possible true function of theatre.

To get to the real heart of the matter, one has to be willing to ask more questions, not to settle for the answer that seems like a complete answer. One could say an audience goes to the theatre to be fed in the form of impressions, and be satisfied with this answer.

One should never be satisfied. Let's delve deeper. Being fed? Why? For what purpose? And if they receive this "food," do they also give it? What is the nature of this food? If it's true that you are what you eat, does that apply to impressions as well? I challenge you to continue to ask: *What is going on here?*

E.J. Gold, *Ah, How Pleasant It Is to Be Wearing a Hat of Stars*, Pen & Ink, 11" x 15", Rives BFK, 1987.

CHAPTER SIX

SLEEP AND THE AWAKENING

Thanks to a number of scientific studies on the levels of human consciousness, we are beginning to be able to make informed comparisons between the "normal" states of awareness. Within the two major ones, sleep and wakefulness, there are sub-categories. In sleep, for example, there are periods of REM sleep (Rapid Eye Movement), deep dreamless sleep, and an assortment of sleep states still under investigation. The waking state is thought to be just that: awake.

There are, of course, more obvious distinctions when dealing with unusual states of consciousness. Trauma, for instance, might induce shock; blood sugar imbalance might bring on dizziness; and stress (depending upon the type of stress) might bring about organic distress such as heart failure or else extraordinary feats of strength, endurance, and mental acuity.

Nearly everyone can relate to the "automatic pilot" state, where suddenly you realize you are home and you don't really recall the drive, or you struggle briefly to remember your own phone number, or you are at a party and even though you are having a good time, there are moments when you catch yourself staring into space. Oddly enough, those states are still lumped in the general "awake" category, considered harmless and a natural part of human consciousness. But what about *awakening*, that cosmic state of awareness described by wise men for eons?

To begin with, consider that the starting premise for nearly all spiritual paths is the recognition that you are totally asleep. Not just spacing out or daydreaming now and then; you are asleep. Just because you may be walking and can talk and even be impressive to others, does not mean that you are necessarily awake. The ordinary state which most people consider to be awake, is, to most spiritual teachers, sleep. It is a somnambulistic existence wherein the person functions in a kind of hazy dream, going from one distraction to another without any real aim or purpose.

The classic formula for awakening is a *profound recognition of the sleep state,* followed by *expert preparation and guidance.* And in truth, the awakened state is not entirely foreign to the seeker who wishes to awaken. Glimpses of it which may have occurred in early childhood, or during an auto accident, or in moments of deep reflection, have alerted the being to a new possibility. It is a state that defies verbal description, but is generally thought of as a timeless, fearless sense of unity and bliss, mixed with a strong intuitive understanding of the cosmic mysteries.

The understanding of the cosmic mysteries usually manifests in the form most suited to the individual. That is, a composer might suddenly understand the laws of creation through his music, a poet through his poetry, a gardener through his gardening, and so on. That is why it is important for people to follow their natural talents, for it is within the framework of their work that the knowledge will be given.

At some point, a guide is needed to help discern between real awakenings and false, imaginary ones. These guides can pace a student's growth to help him or her arrive at his or her highest potential. Their methods are many and each student requires slightly different treatment. So it is useless to try to categorize methods.

There are, however, some basic recurring formats. For example, nearly all teachers start with relaxation. Some concentrate on the breath, others on doing tasks slowly, others rely on massage or visualization journeys. These are all techniques geared toward establishing a ground of relaxation wherein new ways of being are introduced.

Today, everyone recognizes the importance of relaxation in life. In the past few decades, there has been a major impetus to reduce stress in order to maximize health and efficiency. The massive medical establishment has backed the idea 100%. And then—boom! We are inundated with a thousand

and one ways to reduce stress: massage, hot tubs, yoga, meditation, jogging, walking, sensory-deprivation tanks—therapeutic activities galore, not to mention the massive pain relieving and stress reducing drug market, both legal and illegal.

Actors, like everyone else, must deal with stress, sometimes with an inordinate amount. Now, more than ever, they recognize the importance of managing their stress, so that it will not impede the flow of creative energy.

The spiritual quest, however, *induces* stress—not the stress normally associated with pressure in the work-a-day world—similar, but not the same. The adept must undergo a journey of preparation that is the right mix of relaxation and moments of high stress that produce for the being *constructive shocks.*

The shocks, once the natural by-product of living in a primitive environment, must now, due to contemporary buffers, be administered through participation in spiritual work. Some shocks are provided at first by the teacher but are eventually the responsibility of the student. The shock might come in the form of a blasting shout from a Zen master, a sudden and unexpected admonition from a teacher, an emotional crisis that reflects deeply repressed flaws in character, or in countless other forms depending upon the creativity and temperament of the teacher.

These shocks are used to boost the vibrational frequency of the student at properly timed intervals to facilitate a new understanding. The knowledge of when and how much of a shock to administer is a very delicate science and must be provided by only the most qualified teachers. Constructive shocks, if they are to be of any value, usually occur through *the law of necessity*. And a true teacher responds to this law.

That law follows the precept that the cosmos responds readily to real need and is less responsive to desires. An extreme example from life is the story of the woman whose child was accidentally struck and trapped by a car. In an instant, she lifted the car and freed her child. This, of course, is a feat normally impossible for her, or anyone else.[1] Yet, the law of necessity made it possible for her to access powerful, apparently miraculous energy.

By placing the element of necessity into a task, the actor/adept can perform amazing feats. Grotowski made use of this fact when in his early experiments he would ask his actors to dive over their fellow actors who were lying shoulder to shoulder on the mat. The number of actors on the mat gradually increased, forcing the actor to dive farther in order to avoid landing on one of his compatriots.[2] This exercise yielded remarkable feats of physical ability, including the ability to leap over a fellow actor who is standing. These feats are largely due to the law of necessity.

The added dimension of necessity creates, as you can imagine, a very real element of stress, a constructive variety of stress. Once a person consciously and successfully springboards off stress into new territories of awareness and accomplishment, there is no longer any need to intellectualize the difference between sleep and awakening.

An audience can provide such a springboard. Their expectation is a form of stress which most actors enjoy. The stress lifts them above themselves and charges a performance with a palpable wakefulness. During rehearsals, a good director provides a similar stress, as do the other actors. And in reality, it is this combined stress or charge that first hooks people into the theatre, because in the final analysis, it feels wonderful.

Mystery schools and brotherhoods work in groups for the same reasons, using the group energy to activate a field of energy similar to that of an audience. Or they meditate for long periods, achieving stress through enforced periods of concentration or encounters with nothingness. Or they meet face to face with the master teacher and must supply a response to a question or koan. And there are many other "stress factors" used in the spiritual training business.

One important, but little known stress factor, used in some mystery schools, and one that actors could also effectively use, is the *tolerance of negative manifestations of others.* That is to say, simply being in the presence of others who are a source of irritation for you or who provide stressful negative energy, could work to awaken you. The key word in the technique is *tolerate.* You must not be drawn into the negativity, but remain attentive, sensing the effect it has on your organism.

Regarding this, St. Abba Dorotheus, one of the early Desert Fathers from the Benedictine Trappist order, says this:

Over whatever you have to do, even if it be very urgent and demands great care, I would not have you argue or be agitated. For rest assured, everything you do, be it great or small, is but one eighth of the problem, whereas to keep one's state undisturbed even if thereby one should fail to accomplish the task, is the other seven-eighths...If, however, in order to accomplish your task you would inevitably be carried away and harm yourself or another by arguing with him, you should not lose seven for the sake of preserving one eighth.[3]

And really, this is parallel to the teaching of Jesus which asks his followers to "turn the other cheek." However, it takes training and practice to turn the other cheek. And that is another reason why there is emphasis on groups, schools, and monastic orders. Ideally, within those controlled environments, a person can test his ability to turn his cheek on a regular basis until it is authentic.

I am reminded of a story about Roy Hart, a promising young actor studying at the Royal Academy in London years ago. He went to study voice with a teacher named Alfred Wolfsohn, who had a reputation as a particularly gifted teacher. At the first lesson, Roy told Alfred that he was frustrated in acting class because he was working on playing Othello, but could not connect at all with the character, because Othello murders Desdemona and Roy knew he was not a murderer.

Alfred listened and then as the lesson began, he started to insult and berate Roy at every turn. They began to argue at one point whereupon Alfred kept on provoking him until Roy erupted in a violent outburst exclaiming, "I'm going to kill you!" At that point Alfred dropped his attack, smiled, and said, "So, now we see the murderer. It is best to find him in your art, lest he sneak out unexpectedly in life."

Roy went on to study extensively with Alfred, later carrying on his work in the form of a theatre company—The Roy Hart Theatre.

The point is, mastering our flaws, at the deepest level, takes an artistry and technique that must be developed. True and lasting tolerance is the result of transformation over time through the continued exposure to irritants which, by the way, are heightened in a group situation.

For years I thought this was a relatively new technique, used only in the West, until I came across the following quote in the *Annals of the Hall of Blissful Development* by Huang Yuan-chi, a Chinese adept who lived during the Yuan Dynasty. He states:

> People are happy when there is quiet and vexed when there is commotion. Don't they realize that since their energy has already been stirred by the clamor of people's voices and the involvements and disturbances of people and affairs, rather than use this power to be annoyed at the commotion, it is better to use this power to cultivate stability. An ancient said, "When people are in the midst of the disturbance, this is a good time to apply effort to keep independent." Stay comprehensively alert in the immediate present, and suddenly an awakening will open up an experience in the midst of it all that is millions of times better than quiet sitting. Whenever you encounter people making a commotion, whether it concerns you or not, use it to polish and strengthen yourself, like gold being refined over and over again, until it no longer changes color. If you

gain power in this, it is much better than long drawn-out practice in quiet.

I hope you can see the significance of this concept. It not only shatters the myth of needing to retreat to a cave somewhere to meditate alone in quiet, but it implies that staying calm amid the clamor of life, practicing an emotional Tai Chi, is a *million* times more beneficial! And where better than the theatre to find such clamor!

All this insistence on relaxation lately is a good thing if used to counteract the wrong kinds of stress, but it is useless and indeed counterproductive if it diminishes the possibility for constructive stress.

The actor's world is ideally suited for the process of awakening. The problem at present, in my estimation, is the fact that there is no tradition to supply models of progress. In other words, there is no reliable, agreed upon measure of spiritual progress in Western theatre.

In the Eastern theatre, the theatrical form maintained its contact with religious celebrations, shamanistic rain dances, fertility rites, and other rituals. It is a mystic partnership with the forces of the universe and comes with a tradition that keeps tabs on spiritual progress. But that, too, shows signs of erosion.

In today's world, both East and West endure a rapid acceleration of materialism and a fragmented spiritual base. The Japanese no longer rely on Buddhism, Confucianism, or even Shintoism as their primary source of inspiration, and Christianity is losing its luster in the West. The world is, in fact, fast becoming a huge chaotic marketplace. And actors must somehow work within this market.

To the spiritually inclined, the marketplace seems to be the enemy, a distraction pulling them from their highest aims. Not so for the artist who knows not only the value of transmuting the clamor, but the elements of his art that are integral to spiritual awakening.

In acting, for example, training in tolerance of others can begin immediately, with no special instruction. By working for the good of the show, and by tolerating the negative manifestations of others—or even of oneself—one is developing the internal power necessary to do the same in life.

In nearly every cast there will be a typicality that rubs the wrong way, that seems to bring out the beast in you. Yet the irritation must be endured for the sake of the show. This does not imply total impunity for disruptive or dangerous behavior; people who behave that way must be expelled for the good of the whole project. But during the course of working together to make the show work, there are inevitable frictions based on personality conflicts and petty emotional reactions. These feelings that erupt are the fuel for progress. They are actually instrumental in establishing *real presence,* a necessary step toward awakening.

But what is the nature of the awakened state? Why attempt such a change in consciousness at all? Well, that's just it. Most people are content to carry on under the illusion that they are the masters of their lives, to live their lives in semi-darkness and in perpetual existential anguish. They view their quiet suffering as "reality" and think nothing more of it. They try to fill the emptiness with myriad compulsions and sensory stimulation, to no avail. And it is the great vanity of most people that keeps them in darkness, convinced they are already awake.

When, however, due to an unusual shock an accidental awakening occurs and the person gets a glimpse of real human possibility, he or she becomes forever hounded by that potential.

If one can manage to pull away from the rush of daily sensation and cultural demands long enough to begin self-cultivation, the advantages of awakening become increasingly attractive.

There is, however, a slight glitch in the process. It's not all peaches and cream. The automatic part of us, the machine, wants peaches and cream and wants to keep its dominant position as the ruler of the house. There is an inner conflict that has to be dealt with intelligently.

One way is to use the compulsions and hungers of the machine against itself until it learns to accept the awakened state. Regarding this, E.J. Gold, high-tech shaman, transformational psychologist and author of *The Human Biological Machine As A Transformational Apparatus*, says this:

> ...we should realize that, because the machine was not fully awake during these glimpses of awakening, the machine still exerted its will, and because the machine was not fully awake, and vestigial traces of the sleeping state remained somewhat active to a greater or lesser degree, we inevitably experienced some discomfort which would not be part of a complete waking state.

This initial discomfort during the process of entering the waking state from the sleeping state is the principal reason we fall back into the sleeping state...When the machine first comes to life, we may find the experience too excruciating, too emotionally, mentally and physically painful, too exhausting, and we may decide to allow the machine to fall back into sleep.

Eventually if the machine remains in the sleeping state, gangrene will set in and the machine will die. This is the chief cause of ordinary death. If the machine were awake, it would also eventually die, but not in the same way.[4]

So you see, there is ample warning that it may not be entirely pleasant. Yet, anyone who is called to awaken knows deep inside the value of enduring momentary discomfort for the chance to evolve and serve God and His plan for humanity.

In summary, there are a number of things in the theatre which can lend themselves to spiritual refinement, namely: development of the actor's instrument to orchestrate his four bodies (moving, emotional, intellectual, and instinctual); participation in the presentation of quality impressions; creating inner strength by tolerating the negative manifestations of others; channeling archetypes and entities from lower and higher worlds; and, if fully awake, the actor can consciously journey to other realms, giving his work a range and power equalling the master painters, composers, and thinkers of all time. To do this, however, he must develop that which can operate and exist in those realms. That is the subject of my next chapter.

E.J. Gold, *Pierrot de la Lune,*
Pen & Ink, 11" x 15", Rives BFK, 1987.

CHAPTER SEVEN

HIGHER BODIES

As stated earlier, both science and metaphysics agree that reality is a vibratory phenomenon. Itzhak Bentov, in his book, *Stalking the Wild Pendulum,* goes on to state that our physical bodies, which are in essence interacting wave patterns, will inevitably, like all interactive wave patterns, contain higher harmonics (You may recall the example of striking middle C on the piano).

He contends that there exist other "bodies" made up of higher harmonics of our physical body. They, of course, may not look like our physical body, but they exist, vibrating at relative frequencies. Our astral body is one harmonic, the mental another, the causal another, and so on.

He further contends that we are, in a way, a radio-like device receiving four or five different "stations" simultaneously. We can't hear the subtle, non-physical stations, because the physical station is usually blaring. If we manage to quiet the loud station, we can tune in to the higher harmonics.[1]

By tuning in to the higher frequencies, we align our instrument with higher and higher realities. Eventually, and usually only after great struggle and sacrifice, we are given the possibility to actually create "bodies" that correspond to these other realms.

The creation of higher bodies in order to travel and relate to other dimensions is the alchemical process behind most religions, although most of them either keep this idea hidden or have forgotten it. For example, the story of Jesus is essentially the story of how to prepare and complete a higher body—one capable of revealing itself, even after death.

The progression of the bodies is usually described as: Astral, Causal, Intuitive, Mental, Spiritual, and others which I won't include here. This hierarchy of bodies corresponds to the hierarchy of realms. And, as we might expect, there are differing opinions as to the names and qualities of the bodies and realms. That is where contact with a spiritual tradition can be helpful.

For example, the ancient as well as modern Taoists concern themselves almost exclusively with the cultivation of higher bodies—particularly the crystal body, which is sometimes called the diamond body.[2] These bodies if correctly cultivated will result in a balanced and righteous life on earth and conscious immortality. That is to say, instead of death sweeping the soul into the cycle of reincarnation, the integrity of the complete crystal body passes on to a heavenly realm of its own actualization.[3]

For the Taoist, the initial and primary method of cultivation is the collection and proper distribution of chi (or Prana in the Indian system) which is the elemental and invisible life force. Once the meridians of the body have been cleared and cleansed, the chi can begin to collect in preparation to awaken the higher harmonics. In relation to this, here is what Gurdjieff, as reported by Ouspensky, says:

> If the physical organism begins to produce a sufficient quantity of these fine substances [hydrogens], and the "astral body" within it becomes formed, this astral organism will require for its maintenance less of these substances than it needed during its growth. The surplus from these substances can then be used for the formation and growth of the "mental body" which will grow with the help of the same substances that feed the "astral body," but of course the growth of the "mental body" will require more of these substances than the growth and feeding of the "astral body." The surplus...will go to the growth of the fourth body. But in all cases the surplus will have to be large. All the fine substances necessary for the growth and feeding of the higher bodies must be produced within the physical organism, and the physical organism is able to produce them provided the human factory is working properly and economically.[4]

The ever-popular *out of body* experience relates to the ability of the astral form to detach from the body and consciously travel. We of course do this every night in our sleep. But to be conscious of the process and to actually experience this plane of reality in an invisible form, well, that's something else entirely.

There are countless cases cited of this phenomenon, and science, when it deigns to address the issue, is usually unable to take a stand. Nevertheless, there is mounting evidence that the human instrument is indeed capable of such a state.

Brian Bates, a psychologist who spent seven years researching the psychology of acting with students at the Royal Academy of Dramatic Art in London, has done experiments in which he helped guide an actor's consciousness to detach itself and roam around the building, reporting continuously along the way. Although the observations of the traveling actor were uncanny in their detail, and even though the actor afterwards was convinced he had left his body and traveled about the building, Bates still injects a hint of skepticism, implying it might be a hypnotic fantasy, born out of the power of an actor's imagination.[5]

But what is imagination? It strikes me as sad that because we have a name for some function of our being, we assume we understand it. The imagination might be operating under a certain set of laws yet undiscovered.

Light is not really visible until we receive it in the retina—which is a limited, although wonderful, sensor. And we humans are privy to only a certain spectrum of light waves in a vast world of waves. If we rub our eyes we can witness an array of kaleidoscopic effects. What of that? Is it just nerves creating images? Well, how? Why the patterns?

And from where comes the illumination in our dreams? Is this not light? Perhaps it is the memory of light. Even if it is memory, it is perceived as light. And isn't it mind-boggling that a function in the brain can reproduce light which is an energy travelling at 186,000 miles per second? From where does that kind of mental energy originate?

I bring this up because I think settling for "it's only imagination" is avoiding the issue. The actor/shaman has the ability to develop contact with the deepest, most mysterious parts of the human soul. Having the powers of imagination and concentration that actors have is obviously a pre-requisite for conscious out-of-body experiences.

Such experiences are a natural, albeit unconscious, occurrence in everyone. It is the artist conscious of this voyaging function, however, who gives hope for man's spiritual development. The powers learned in acting are an ideal preparation.

Having powers, however, does not imply having success; success meaning *having created that which lasts beyond the veil.* Having the tools does not mean that one has the plan. One must have both. And to work properly, avoiding mistakes that could be very serious, one needs a guide.

An out of body experience, for example, although certainly thrilling to the traveler, is not necessarily evidence of having created an astral body. One needs expert coaching in these matters and above all, an honest aim. Formulating a true aim outside the usual curiosity-seeking mentality will protect the voyager from harm. Remember: *aim is everything.*

E.J. Gold, *Harlequin of Lesser Birds*,
Pen & Ink, 11" x 15", Rives BFK, 1987.

CHAPTER EIGHT

HIGHER PURPOSE

Most of the recent teachings getting popular exposure lately, by healers, channelers, and some schools, have one recurring basic directive in common: they all ask you to love yourself. Loving yourself, they say, will begin to heal blocks and bring you gently into a more powerful, balanced state of being.

While noble in intent and certainly valuable in today's world where people are forever falling prey to low self-esteem, there is a danger. This danger is exemplified by the ancient Hebrew legend of Balaam. According to the legend, Moses was for a time a fugitive in the camp of the King of Ethiopia. The King was in the odd position of besieging his own capital because it had been taken over by the unrighteous sorcerer Balaam, who used his powers to influence others without the integrity of the spirit. Balaam represents that part of the psyche that seeks power without reference to anything higher than self-love.[1]

One must, of course, have a degree of self-esteem to tackle the acting world and still feel called to spiritual service. The service, however, must be rooted in something higher than the self or one steps across the boundary into what is commonly known as black magic. And as a teacher of mine once reminded me: black magicians die like dogs.

Higher purpose implies something larger, something beyond the small self. It also reiterates the idea that creation is modular—systems are contained within larger systems[2]—and that by changing the frequency of energy fields, we can interact with other systems. Higher purpose, then, is related to contacting and in some way serving a larger or higher energy field. This we normally call God.

Using Bentov's model, human consciousness is being stimulated to grow to the level where it can allow its sophisticated body of knowledge to be absorbed by a giant information bank. Like cosmic reporters who are reporting *on* the creation *to* the creation which *is* the creator. Or as Shankara, the Indian philosopher, says:

> *On the vast canvas of the Self*
> *the picture of the manifold worlds*
> *is painted by the Self itself.*
> *And that Supreme Self*
> *seeing but itself,*
> *enjoys great delight.*

E.J. Gold's model is the same, only he takes it one step further and suggests that the Supreme Self cannot properly see itself because it has been ensnared by its own creation, forced as it were by the whole process to doze. Man's purpose then is to awaken the endless creator, the Absolute, by awakening himself and thus alleviating the suffering of the Absolute.

Wait a minute, you say? To do what? Alleviate the suffering of the Absolute? How on earth can the Absolute suffer? That is a bonus question if I've ever heard one, and I am not going to give my version of an answer and thereby steal that task from you. Suffice it to say that most religions adhere to a notion of God's suffering—the crucifixion of Jesus being the obvious example—in which man has a role to play by either alleviating that suffering or being redeemed by it.

These ideas may be burdensome at first, I know. And clearly, not everyone is capable or called to participate directly in such service. Some actors can take solace in knowing that their experiences are valuable and their very being is a great and useful contribution to the collective hologram of knowledge being assembled by God.

But for those who can see little joy in life as it is, who want to participate in the struggle for evolution—well, there may be work ahead.

A good way for an actor to begin to discover true higher purpose is by cultivating compassion towards character. Like a puppeteer who has the compassion to animate and give life to something inanimate, the actor can give life to a character which is dead, nothing but words on a page.

As the character grows, the actor must begin to identify with and actually sympathize with the entire character, even the ugly or negative aspects. This act of opening up to the character, loving it, seeing the frailties and faults, playing the truth of the character unconditionally, is an act of profound compassion.

To surrender to the character, *with no craving for reward,* is essential. It can begin the process of dissolving the ordinary need for reward and establish a new frame of reference for work—one that is not dependent on the reward system.

And by doing this, one can overcome Balaam, one can recognize the gifts that already exist and pay the debt to the universe by becoming ready to aid in the work of unification, which is redemption.

This service, sacrifice, aid, whatever you want to call it, is the key to establishing higher purpose. Keep in mind that because of the wide variety of souls and paths, your higher purpose may not be suited for anyone else but you. And as such, attempts to convert others are very often a transference of insecurity ("Gee, if I get enough people to believe like me, then I can truly believe!").

With dedication and guidance, the actor has the opportunity to resonate with higher entities, accumulate data, and experience the kind of awareness normally reserved for saints and sages. That is not to imply that everyone will do so. In fact, as a result of humanity's slumber there are very few people who will attempt a path of self-cultivation and fewer still who will manage actually to achieve anything of consequence. Nevertheless, there is hope, and grace, and possibility for actors to serve a higher purpose and in so doing, to sanctify their art.

E.J. Gold, *The Stars Are My Thoughts,*
Pen & Ink, 11" x 15", Rives BFK, 1987.

CHAPTER NINE

MINDFULNESS

> To be fully conscious in all situations and condi-
> tions of life, is what the Buddha meant when he said
> we should be mindful while sitting, standing, lying
> down, or walking. But 'fully conscious' does not
> mean to be conscious of only one aspect or function
> of our body, or our mind, but to be conscious with
> and of our whole being, which includes body and
> mind and something that goes beyond body and
> mind: namely that deeper reality at which the Bud-
> dha hinted in the term *Dharma* and which he realized
> in the state of Enlightenment.[1]
>
> —*Lama Govinda*

If you have studied acting, the following
description may be familiar to you: You are working
on a sense awareness exercise in acting class. The
instructor tells you not to generalize the feeling of
the sun on your body, but to sense where the exact
highlights are and to let that inform your entire

instrument. Or how about this one: the instructor asks you just to breathe and simply be aware of the breath going in and out, perhaps saying a poem or a few lines from a play as you do this. Maybe you have been asked to stand in front of the class and say your ABC's with no inflection, trying to find a neutral place. Or if your class is geared to a more active dynamic, the instructor may have you walking around the room, leading with different areas of the body and observing the feelings associated with the different postures. You may be surprised to know that these and countless other acting exercises are variations of an ancient meditation practice called Mindfulness.

The meditation is associated most often with Buddhism, particularly Japanese Zen. But there are similar practices in most other religions as well. The apparent motive for such exercises, in religion as well as theatre, is to focus the attention. The results vary according to the ultimate aim of the practice. Generally, however, it is to calm the habitual chatter of the mind and gradually to develop insight.[2]

The starting point in most Buddhist-based practices is the mindfulness of breath. The adept sits in a posture that allows the spine to be straight and the balance to be "locked," avoiding any sudden movements or falling. Then the mind rests at the belly around the navel and simply watches or in some cases counts the breath.

I have experienced this, sitting in zazen every morning for a year, and although it sounds simple, it is not. The mind wants to scatter and resists the intention just to sit and focus. However, after a while, with gentle persistence, the mind will give in to the calm and a very satisfying peace spreads throughout the being.

A similar kind of peace is attained in moving meditations like the Chinese Tai Chi Chuan. Once the movement sequence is learned, the breath and subtle energy flows as part of a smooth undisturbed meditation. The added benefit of doing Tai Chi is that it generates a healthy life force and maintains the body in a fit, yet flexible, shape.

Although certainly useful for many people in providing a break from the hyper pace of modern living, the mindfulness practices in their Eastern forms are often less useful for the actor. Tai Chi will help relax the actor and help focus the mind and, of course, that is useful. But it can make some performers too soft, too gentle in their approach to their work. By the same token, a sitting meditation (as in half or full lotus), can weaken and in some cases seriously damage the knees. And even though there are positive effects of that kind of concentration, it is often inappropriate for someone whose energy needs to be theatrically viable.

So how should an actor practice mindfulness? Let me begin by telling you a story. While living in New York some years back, I took some acting classes from the American actor Michael Moriarty. His beginning technique was very close to Zen meditation, although I didn't recognize it as such at the time. It was called the Players' Acting Technique.

In this technique, an actor would come to class, sit in a chair and read a text, quietly, gently allowing the breath to be the underlying guide to unlocking the subconscious. One day, I read a monologue which was a satirical piece about a character whose spiritual practices were so numerous and time-consuming, he never got out of the house. After the critique, Michael spoke briefly about his own experience of searching for God.

He said that for two years he went to the Zen Center there in New York and sat, somewhat miserably, in the lotus position and meditated. Then suddenly, it came to him one day as he was sitting in his anguish, searching for truth. He thought, "I am an actor, and an actor must find truth in all positions."

That thought freed him and brought him back into the theatre with renewed vigor. And when he told this to the class, it freed me, too. I still meditate and do Tai Chi, but the practice of mindfulness in my life extends beyond those Eastern forms. As indeed it should.

Essentially, Mr. Moriarty was saying that it is not so much the *what,* as the *how.* I can, for example, write these words or any words and it can be automatic, or a meditation, depending on how I approach it.

The actor must learn from these Eastern techniques and digest what they have to offer, but for this learning to be integrated into acting, the principles must leave the Zafu pillow and move into the theatre.

Fortunately, there are thoroughly Western techniques which can help accomplish just that. The Alexander Technique, for example, widely used in training actors in Britain, Canada, and the U.S., is very close to being what I would call Western Zen.

F. Matthias Alexander was a pioneer in the concept of mind-body unity. He developed his theories in the last decade of the nineteenth century and then taught until his death in 1955. It would take volumes to illuminate the breadth of his work and influence. Obviously, therefore, I cannot present a full-scale analysis of his system.

I will, however, mention a few key elements of his technique which parallel techniques used in Zen training. First and foremost is his concept of the head/neck connection. He saw the direction and placement of the head as it relates to the neck as being of fundamental importance to the optimum functioning of the organism.[3]

While Zen does not necessarily find that connection to be of paramount value, his directions for the student to place the mind there while monitoring changes within and without is very close to another Buddhist insight meditation known as Vipassana.

In Vipassana, the meditator places his attention on his breath, or on a part of the body, maintaining a gentle but continuous focus on that part. The Alexander technique simply takes the view that the body part should be the place where the head connects with the neck.

There are other similarities: In Zen, there is the idea of mastering the balance and awareness in the four basic postures—sitting, standing, lying down, and walking. Initial Alexander work begins with just these same postures. And afterwards, Zen teaches that essential mindfulness and grace should be applied to all the activities of the day, regardless how mundane. On this, Alexander himself says:

The essence of the religious outlook is that religion should not be kept in a compartment by itself, but that it should be the ever-present guiding principle underlying the "daily round," the "common task." So also it is possible to apply this principle of life in the daily round of one's activities without involving a loss of attention in these activities.[4]

Being attentive to the postural relationship of the body to gravity, and using thought to redirect habitual patterns of movement, is an activity requiring presence in the moment. The monitoring and re-learning throughout the day create a fresh mental awareness with a graceful physical ease. This is pure Zen.

This is not to imply that the process is entirely without effort. We are creatures of forgetfulness and the effort to *remember* to balance the head and to redirect the actions of sitting, walking, and so on, takes a good deal more fortitude than you might think. The experience of internal composure that accompanies alignment, however, establishes an appetite for that composure and eventually makes the remembering easier.

Another parallel between Zen practice and Alexander technique is the concept of *inhibition*. Alexander used the concept, not in the sense of thwarting desire or suppression, but in reference to by-passing habitual modes of thinking and doing.[5] He discovered that once the thought to do something happened, such as deciding to stand from a sitting position, the nervous system charged a particular set of nerves in preparation. This set of nerves was invariably the habitual pattern which had been learned according to compulsion, conditioning, and what Alexander called, "the wrong sense of what's right."

Therefore, in a lesson, the Alexander teacher might tell the student to tell herself she is not going to stand—and then to stand up. This way, she inhibits the original impulse to stand, which allows for a new pattern to be learned.

Paul Reps, at the end of his book *Zen Flesh/Zen Bones* includes a list of practices and meditations. One of them is clearly the directive of inhibition. It says: "Just as you have the impulse to do something—stop."

Finally, one of the key elements in Zen is non-attachment, particularly to result. Attachment to result is really the same thing as Alexander's term, *end gaining*. Alexander used this concept to describe people who used their will to hammer their way towards a desired end, with little to no concern for the means. The end gainer insists on the process simply "feeling right." The problem here is that whatever activity the end gainer is doing, he has a misdirected use of his instrument. Therefore, improvement and excellence is nearly impossible. Feeling right, in this case, is a deterrent to learning.[6]

As stated earlier, Alexander was a pioneer in this field. Since his time, there have been an ever-growing number of teachers and researchers who have advanced the knowledge to a remarkable degree. Still, Alexander's fundamental techniques are the most widely used, especially in the theatre.

There is one outstanding practice I should mention, and that is the work of Moshe Feldenkrais. His

Awareness Through Movement and Fundamental Integration techniques are fast becoming the next wave in this field. His work has already been enthusiastically endorsed by Peter Brook, and numerous theatre schools in Europe employ Feldenkrais practitioners to help train their actors.

I do not have as much experience with the Feldenkrais method, but I will say that judging from what I experienced during a week-long workshop with Moshe Feldenkrais in New York a few years ago, this man's work may very well be the greatest contribution to the body-mind field to date.

As for its possible relation to mindfulness or the spiritual dimension of acting, I can only relay a statement that I think is very telling. At one point during the workshop that week, Moshe said, "Even if you absorb all the psychological systems in the world, you will accomplish nothing until you change your relationship to time."

The actor works in the medium of time. Condensed moments, comic timing, pauses, silences, pacing, tempo—these are just a few of the elements of time an actor must master. To master those elements implies being free of them as well. Mindfulness is a primary method of finding this freedom. In true mindfulness, time is elastic, unfixed, and playful—allowing for a freshness, a fluidity, that audiences desperately want to experience.

Traditionally, there are four steps in the practice of *right mindfulness* (called *satipatthana* by the Buddhists). One very powerful step is to overcome fear of death by dropping sensual attachment to the body. To do this, the adept must view his own body as a corpse in some stage of decay. He must strongly visualize and consciously face the reality of his eventual death and decay. This is the *reflection on the states of the body* step. There is also the reflection on the states of feeling, the states of mind, and the states of things.[7]

I mention this because there are many times in an actor's life when he will be called upon to die. Meryl Streep apparently went deep into this mystery for a scene in the film *Ironweed;* the crew and the director were actually concerned that she had indeed died![8] Sarah Bernhardt slept in a coffin—no doubt to shed fear of death and bring life into sharper focus. And a great number of Shakespeare's plays have people dropping right and left. Not to mention the majority of modern television and film.

What a perfect opportunity to confront fear of death and to go deeply into it, even as a Buddhist monk would do. These opportunities given to actors are profound meditations in some religious orders. And the actor has been given the possibility to use these not only to enhance his art, but also to establish his momentum on the spiritual path. This is accomplished, in part, by shedding fears and vanities while maintaining an unfailing vigilance over the states of his personality through right mindfulness.

In summary, the actor wanting to find one way to begin working should consider the uses of mindfulness. It can be applied in nearly all areas of actor training: postural alignment, breath release/control, timing, physical characterization, death scenes, and the simple awareness of the moment at hand while performing virtually any task. The real beauty of it

is that it engenders honest, centered spontaneity—
something every actor can put to good use. In mindfulness, then, for the actor, the means is the result!

E.J. Gold, *The Beginning,* Pen & Ink,
11" x 15", Rives BFK, 1987.

CHAPTER TEN

GATEWAYS

One need not be a seeker long before discovering that the variety of "ways" or "paths" number in the thousands. Each way protects its own system and although there are sects and orders which recognize and support other approaches, most define themselves in opposition to the others.

In Christianity for example, there are many branches of faith within the original Roman Catholic Church. There is, for example, a wide variety of orders of monks and nuns. The Episcopal Church is nearly identical in ritual, but does not adhere to Papal authority. The Protestant reformation produced a multitude of churches, each with its own unique character and approach.

And similar branching has occurred with every major and minor religious path in the world. It is as if a mathematical equation is at work, an equation that parallels closely the structure governing the growth of trees, families, even ideas. It seems that religion, like nature, follows the route toward increased specialization and refinement.

Also, it is evident that nearly all primary religions center around a core figure or hero who either arrives with or attains godlike stature, for example, Jesus, Buddha, Mohammed, Zeus, Moses, Shiva, and so on. Some religions are adamant about their way being the *only* or the *right* way. And indeed, the respective Godheads insist on fidelity to their religions. They warn against getting involved with the heathens, pagans, barbarians, cannibals, witches, or devils that inhabit the other houses of worship.

When I was younger, I was greatly repulsed by the "private club" mentality of most religions. Later, as I progressed on my "pathless path," I recognized this separative posture as a necessary part of all religious orders. As a congregation or group is formed, they become, in essence, a cellular entity. They must create protective membranes to secure the integrity of their structure. The process of doing that often involves the rejection of other cellular structures.

Although it may appear unfair or unnecessary, the simple fact is, it *is* necessary. Why? Because the way is straight and narrow!

Joseph Campbell, in his televised interview with Bill Moyers, made a lovely modern analogy to describe this very ancient idea. He compared religions to software packages on a computer. Each personal computer is linked to the main terminal—

or God. However, each software package has its own code, and it is only after learning the code that you can eventually access the main terminal. Dabbling in software is interesting, but it can't take you very far unless you stay with one format.

The defining of a method or religion in opposition to other methods is really motivated by the knowledge that seekers are curious, and if they aren't prodded to stay on one course, they will wander off, dabbling in the glittering software market.

As usual, this essential concept is lost or ignored and before too long there are those who fervently believe the other methods are not only to be avoided, but hated or destroyed. This gives rise to horrible rifts that invite bloodshed, persecution, paranoia, and war.

The reason people become hateful is usually related to power. For some odd reason, we humans seem to feel that dominance over other humans will in some way secure immortality. In this way, hunger for power (manifesting as greed, lust, cruelty and murder) is related to fear of death.

Real power, power that is not related to fears of dying, is a power described by most religions as a true inner peace—an understanding of one's place in the universe. People who have no inner peace, who ignore their possible place or suspect that there is no such thing, sense a deep weakness or hunger inside that must be constantly bolstered and fed.

I have known performers like this. They must have constant reinforcement of their worth. They are desperate for acceptance and in a misguided attempt to satisfy their desperation, they will often sacrifice the intimacy that they truly need for applause. I have also known others who for a variety of reasons confidently knew their worth. Without resorting to puffery, they could accept the love of an audience as well as that of friends and intimates.

These performers with real inner power have what is often referred to as *presence*. There is a noticeable radiance about them. It is not by chance that famous performers are described as "luminaries" or "stars." In esoteric terms, they have developed their internal power to the degree that they can activate what is known as *radiance.*

There are different levels of radiance similar to different levels of light. The radiance of a "healthy glow," for example, is a low level but recognizable light. The "after glow" of sexual intercourse is a slightly higher level light, but still low when compared with the bright light of a sexual climax. Some actors beam onstage, others might glow, and still others, albeit only a few, seem to blast with radiance; one can't stop watching them.

Many Indian Gurus are said to emit a radiant light. It is believed to be beneficial just to be in the presence of such *enlightened* energy. Ram Dass, teacher and author of *Grist for the Mill* and *Be Here Now,* tells of how his Guru maintained a flow of light that emanated a steady warmth and love-filled radiance enjoyed by anyone in his immediate circle of influence. This vibration from an advanced being can work to elevate the spiritual possibility of an entire community—that is why in India, Yogis who may do nothing else but sit in deep blissful meditation are considered valuable. They are supported by the enthusiastic contributions of the community.

Radiance, especially of the face, is considered by many faiths to be a sign of spiritual attainment. Taoists, for example, are characteristically methodical in their evaluations. For them, if the facial light is pure and white, it means that one has attained mental energy and strengthened one's lungs. If the face is a radiant black, one's kidneys are strong and one has benefit from the firmness of one's essences. If the radiance is a strong yellow, the person has pure chi or life force.[1]

In the Bible, there are many examples of radiance. Moses, coming down with the two Tables of Testimony, showed facial radiance because "he had been speaking with the Lord" (Exodus 34:29). And there are many accounts of halos and auras which could be perceived by ordinary people.

Taken in individual terms, when a person reaches a certain level of enlightenment, he or she can rise from the mundane state of the body to the level of the upper worlds. The greater the duration and exposure to the upper worlds, the deeper and longer the radiance remains.[2]

I have had some experience with radiance and have witnessed examples of extraordinary luminescence in some beings. Although I understood radiation and knew of its existence in spiritual circles, imagine my surprise when I read Michael Chekhov's book, *To the Actor,* and discovered that he not only recognized its existence, but was explaining the phenomenon as it relates to acting technique!

In his book, he instructs the student to imagine rays shooting out from different parts of the body. He asks them to fill the space with their radiation, imagining that the air around them is filled with light. Then, to my amazement, he gives further instruction which might be a lecture to Tibetan monks in the Himalayas. He says:

> You must not be disturbed by doubts as to whether you are actually radiating or whether you are only imagining that you are. If you sincerely and convincingly imagine that you are sending out rays, the imagination will gradually and faithfully lead you to the real and actual process of radiating.
>
> A sensation of the actual existence and significance of your *inner being* will be the result of this exercise. The use of outer expressions alone is glaring evidence of how some actors forget or ignore that the characters they portray have living souls, and that these souls can be made manifest and convincing through powerful *radiation*.[3]

That hidden aspects of reality can become manifest, is one of the most fundamental secrets of mystic science and the cornerstone of nearly all religions. It follows that man's ability to imagine something with sincere faith is a key to actualizing. And to create radiance through imagination further implies that the upper worlds are accessed through the power of visualization. And that the upper worlds are responsive to that power and manifest energies in this sphere in accordance with man's thoughts.

Whoa now! Take a breath! That means that we participate in creation and that our world is indeed the product of our strongest beliefs. (In this perspective, John Lennon's song *Imagine* is a teaching, not just a "gee, wouldn't it be nice" message). If we can access the upper worlds through great dedication and sacrifice, as did all the great saints and sages of the world, what do we access without great dedication and sacrifice?

I am baiting the question unnecessarily. We of course access lower worlds. Most of us are conditioned to think of lower as grotesque, menacing, and diabolical. And that may be right. Nevertheless, all the evidence points to the fact that we humans are composed of lower and higher energies. Some religions faction the being by negating the lower and striving to become the higher. Others recognize the lower as necessary force, needing to be mastered before attempting the higher. Still others ignore the whole issue, saying that it's the duality of the mind playing tricks again by inventing concepts like "higher" or "lower." Nevertheless, it seems evident that the composition of energy filtered within the human instrument correlates to a variety of realms.

Miracles are results of interfacing between realms. A person saturated with the radiation of cosmic dimensions has certain paranormal powers. In the Hindu tradition, some of these powers manifest as bizarre feats of endurance. There are other powers, commonly called *Siddhis,* that are by-products of advanced training in transcendental Yoga. Some of the Siddhi powers are clairvoyance, weightlessness—the power to control the earth's attraction to the body by developing the opposite (centripedal) tendency—leaving one's body and re-entering it at will, supernormal hearing, and mental telepathy.[4]

The Taoists claim similar powers such as insight into the subtle laws of the universe, flying, telekinesis, and control of the forces of weather.

There are in other religions claims of great healing powers, walking on hot coals, living to be 200 years old, speaking with angelic beings, and raising the dead—to name only a few. These powers may exist and then again they may be empty carrots leading the adept who is attracted to power into self-cultivation which eventually dissolves that attraction.

As far as acting is concerned, there are some definite tangible powers—perhaps not as dynamic as the ones claimed by the Eastern religions, but certainly more verifiable.

The most widely used power for actors is the power of transformation. To be able to *become* another, to consciously surrender to a different set of rhythms, values, and attitudes, is beyond the normal capacity of most people. There is also the power of animal magnetism, whereby the performer can attract and arouse the audience. Marilyn Monroe is a case in point. The ability to capture and hold the attention of others is another power, as is the ability to visualize imagery so clearly, the audience can actually perceive it. For instance, I once saw Marcel Marceau portray an old man in an attic, dancing with his deceased wife's dress. I, and everyone else I spoke with afterwards, perceived him as dancing with a *red satin* dress.

The ability to radiate is also a power. It can stimulate appeal on many levels and certainly makes for effective stage presence. But mature actors know how to regulate their radiance in composition with the other actors on stage. This is a sacrifice of sorts in favor of the higher ideal of ensemble acting. It also serves to maintain harmony among the cast, who are all regulating in favor of the entire show outshining any one performance.

Having power, then, is not everything. True wisdom comes with the discretion of when not to use the power. And indeed, the phrase "Not my will, but thy will be done" most certainly applies to paranormal powers.

Moses, it is said, put a veil over his face. He screened his inner radiance with the mask of the ego. This served not only to keep coarser levels from entering, but also to prevent his inner light from blinding others. This was a compassionate act, because when in the presence of a great being, the discrepancies of one's own nature become heightened by contrast which can be a very painful experience. Therefore a teacher often instructs from behind a veil.[5]

Which brings me to the subject of teachers. There is an old adage that says, "When the student is ready, the teacher will appear." I think that is true. It has certainly been the situation in my life. There is also the old adage that says, "seek and ye shall find"—which is also true.

The problem for most people is stepping off the merry-go-round. In the momentum of organic life there seems to be a strange conspiracy against finding the truth. Once that obstacle is overcome, or even as part of overcoming it, a teacher will be there.

Of course, no teacher is right for everyone. And sometimes there are numerous quasi-teachers that must be passed through; they function as tests in sincerity. And sometimes, especially early on, one is given the chance to choose a teacher.

There are many factors to weigh when choosing a teacher. First and foremost, the teacher should be someone who can catch you in your games, who can challenge your masks (something that may not always be pleasant). The teacher must be accomplished in a tradition; must speak to your soul and not your pocketbook; and, ideally, should be accessible, living near enough for daily visits if need be.

Of course, there are all levels of teachers performing a variety of functions. Some teachers work to evoke adoration, which is dormant in most people. The adoration of the teacher is actually a *sadhana* or practice until the student is open and mature enough to make the realization that the teacher is a reflection of something greater. At that point, the student is free of his or her attachment and progresses very fast.

Other teachers might be stern, demanding, and almost militant. This type of teacher supplies the will necessary to carry the green student until he or she has developed a will of his or her own. This approach is stoic and appeals to students who need the feeling of intense challenge.

There are also teachers of the trickster variety who are there to prod, confuse, and delight the student. In this model, the student occasionally gets glimpses of the radiance of the teacher, but the trickster changes too rapidly for the student to form definite attachments. Eventually the student gives up the rational grasping mode and opens to experiences that are perceived directly by the soul.

Whatever the style, and each teacher will be astonishingly unique, they should know the terrain of the spiritual path well enough to guide a student safely to his or her own discoveries. There are some teachers who are teaching for the wrong reasons. They may be satisfying a need for domination over others, they may be hiding from their own failures, or what is worse, they may have hypnotized themselves into believing they are enlightened.

In my experience, true teachers are not afraid of their organic undies. That is to say, they are not struggling to portray a saintly image for the sake of the student. They are entirely themselves. They will show compassion and humor when it serves the teaching. They will also test the student's sincerity. But, they will never allow themselves to be the victim of the student's projected images of them. Nor will they abuse their power or display punitive measures of dominance. And ultimately, they defy any and all definitions of themselves.

Eventually, each seeker becomes his or her own teacher. However, there is rarely a spiritual path that does not stress the importance of proper guidance, especially in the beginning. Upon finding a teacher, one's personal sense of discernment should be the deciding factor. Keep in mind that many of the great teachers veil their radiance, so you cannot go by their "presence" alone.

But why should actors find a teacher at all? Haven't I been suggesting that the spiritual elements are in the art of acting? So who needs a teacher?

Yes, the elements are in the art. However, to learn how to orchestrate those elements with exact knowledge you will need a teacher's help. There is no "generic path" to realization. The need for a teacher comes at different times for everyone. Some need it early on, others only much later. But all the signs point to the necessity of a true teacher somewhere along the way. If you find a teacher who has some experience with acting, well, all the better.

Unfortunately, the odds right now are against finding someone with a theatrical background. They are out there, just few and far between. So actors needing advanced spiritual instruction must weave themselves into a tradition far enough to receive the guidance. And fortunately, most teachers will work within the framework of each student's personal artistry.

Until a teacher manifests, there is help along the way in other forms. One of these I call "divinatories." They are simply one or more of the scores of methods used to "divine" or give "readings" for seekers. The most widely known methods are astrology, palmistry, and the Tarot. There are hundreds more, some of them so fantastic as to border on the absurd. Phrenology, for example, is a practice in which a specialist feels the bumps and shapes of the cranium to determine individual aptitudes. There is also Pyromancy—prediction of the future by means of fire; Geomancy—prediction by means of earth; Hydromancy—prediction by means of water; Aeromancy—prediction by means of the air; Sternomancy—prediction by means of consultation of the area of the body occupied by the sternum; Stoicheiomancy—divination by randomly opening a book and taking the first paragraph on the page as an answer to an already formulated question; Theriomancy—prediction by means of the movements of animals; and Capnomancy—prediction by the movement of smoke, and on and on ad infinitum.[6]

I dare say one could take any format, add the suffix "-mancy," and there would evolve a system of divination. I'm not being facetious. I think that because our material reality is primarily holographic—that is, every part is at the same time the whole—and given the ability of the human receptors to access a variety of realms, including the realms outside our world of time, any device can be used for divination.

Personally, my experiences with such matters were in conventional forms. It was a little overwhelming at first to have a "reading" that was so completely on target, I suddenly felt naked. At the same time, it was liberating. Even when events unfolded exactly as the cards or the astrologer said they would, there were always variations on the basic theme, dictated by my free will.

For a beginning actor, divinatories can bring to light hidden talents and help in career guidance. However, as you begin to know yourself more completely, the need for divination becomes reduced. Life itself becomes the divination.

For the true seeker, the teacher, the powers, the practices, the group dynamics, divinations—virtually everything presents itself as a gateway. Recognizing when the gates are open, however, is a subtle mastery needing great patience and vigilance. Go slowly, as if your life depended on it.

Assume for now that we access both worlds. Are we accessed by both as well? Some say we are. In the Sufi tradition, it is taught that we are invoking some entity all the time, unconsciously. These are like a multitude of masks that flicker across the mirror of our being. Most of them have become crystallized by the conformity to social structures. When invoked involuntarily, each one assumes it is master of the house, unable to admit there are other masks just around the corner.

If you want to witness a mask change sometime, just insult someone. That's the easiest device because human vanity is so fragile. I guarantee you will see a flicker and a new mask will emerge, completely unrelated to the previous one. Even better, try to catch your own masks. The difficulty here is that each mask assumes mastery. The mask that is reading this may indeed vow to be watchful, but before long, a new mask will slip in imperceptibly, and it knows nothing of this vow. The mask that remembers will drift to the depths, only to surface much later when the best opportunities for observation are past.

What is to be done? For the actor, it is easier because he usually works in groups. Group dynamics are such that others can begin to recognize the masks, dissolving their power. Also, the necessity to maintain character, to establish a working set of masks constructed for the portrayal of that being requires a concentration and focus of attention which will facilitate more voluntary participation in the play of one's "own" masks. Then, at some point, masks can actually be used to climb up or down the energy ladder like a totem pole, accessing various realms and accumulating data.

When this is accomplished, there is true liberation from all the masks of creation. At this level, one becomes the Golden Buddha, sitting by the river laughing and changing masks with glee, radiating brightly. All things become possible because all realms have merged in the One Being.

E.J. Gold, *Arlequine,* Pen & Ink,
11" x 15", Rives BFK, 1987.

CHAPTER ELEVEN

SEXUAL ENERGY AND ACTING

It doesn't take a lot of research to discover that the overwhelming majority of dramatic material deals with love, particularly romantic love. There are other themes such as honor, revenge, political struggle, and the like. Upon close inspection, you'll find that even those themes involve love relationships of one kind or another.

I think it can safely be said that more than a few actors have been seduced into the world of acting by their quest for romantic love. Most actors realized early on that they were usually more desirable while performing in a show than when they were not. This, no doubt, added additional fuel to their ambitions to improve their craft. They were literally hot to get cast!

It's also a well known fact that some people are rather plain in the light of everyday, but on stage they glow with a transcendental beauty. Others, perhaps, take a magnificent camera closeup. And some actors seem to get more attractive, more virile, more vibrant as they mature. What is their secret?

It's no secret really. It is just the elusive obvious once again. If you look around today, you will see that the modus operandi for nearly all advertising is sex. What is it the tabloids want most to divulge? Sexual secrets! Everywhere, especially here in the West, there is an extraordinary preoccupation with sex.

Ironically, there is also an extraordinary ignorance surrounding the subject. More often than not, sex is either pure titillation or taboo. And now, with the advent of AIDS, sex has become a "medical issue" full of clinical dangers and fear. An epidemic of enormous proportions has begun to infiltrate humanity. Wisely, people are beginning to screen their partners, take special precautions during sex, and in some cases—abstain altogether.

In the wake of all this, love scenes for actors are now even more complex than ever before. In the back of their minds, they now must ask themselves, "Is it safe?...has this person contracted the disease and if so...what do I do?" This fear, regardless of the evidence that points to AIDS being transmitted only through very specific means (shared needles, blood transfusions, and sexual emission) will no doubt continue to loom.

Actors, who consciously or unconsciously have long relied upon the energy of sex to motivate, elevate, and beautify themselves, are facing a strange dilemma. How do they deal with the new sexual trends and still maintain the open channel to sensuality, intimacy, and bliss?

The first step is to deal consciously with sexual energy. Most people are either prudish (hoping sexual desire will somehow mind its manners), or promiscuous (rebelling against prudishness by over-indulging in sexual passion). Both of these approaches are extremes which can harm the system and ultimately deter progress in many spheres.

Those who hope to control their sexual desire through denial make the unfortunate mistake of fanning the flames by reverse psychology. By virtue of the effort needed to deny the desire, it only sub-limates and grows stronger, needing again more effort and attention from both the conscious mind and the unconscious. This cycle, as Freud pointed out, if left uninterrupted can and often does result in psychological leaks, sometimes called *neurosis*.

At the other extreme, people with an overly active sexual life get trapped in a cycle of ever-increasing thresholds of pleasure and find that they need more and more stimulation. Typically, this cycle of lust leads to emotional knots that are terribly complicated. All of this results in the depletion of vital energies—energies needed to refine, prepare, and activate the spiritual self.

Remember the old adage, *fight fire with fire?* The ancients knew what this meant. They knew that spiritual attainment was only possible after the flaming horses of sexual energy were harnessed. Their secret was to use sexual energy in a conscious manner to enhance their work on higher spiritual centers. They knew that sexual energy helps man rise above sexual energy![1]

How this is done is the focus of a number of spiritual disciplines, Tantra and Yoga being the most widely known. Both systems have undeniable merit and can certainly succeed in the transmutation of sexual energy to serve higher aims. However, my experience with Tantra, in its Indian form, suggests to me a symbolism and discipline too complex to be assimilated by someone who is not a renunciate and fully devoted to the form. Yoga (I refer here primarily to Hatha Yoga) is simpler and more accessible, but I find the accent on breath makes students a little spacey.

So far, for me, the best system is the Taoist system. It is simple, effective, and utilizes sexual energy in a way that is directly applicable to actors. The practices can be done anywhere, without drawing undue attention. Also, the Taoist style of energy circulation sharpens the mind and deepens the contact with both the physical instrument and the emotional body. And finally, it is non-dogmatic and essentially non-religious, allowing the actor to practice the techniques without being drawn into complex religious training.

The Chinese system is very practical and although ceremonial Taoist rites do indeed exist for those who want that aspect, the working ingredients of the system are contained in a relatively simple format, free of myth and ritual. The Chinese also value mastery in the fields of medicine, painting, calligraphy, martial arts, music, poetry, and dance, all of which may be linked to the Taoist system if the adept so desires.

The first part of the format is a meditation technique. The technique is primarily concerned with accumulating "chi" or what we might call "vital force," and then directing the energy along the main energy channels in the body. Typically, the channels are blocked in places and the chi cannot flow. The meditations are used to gradually open them. Once the chi is flowing freely, circulating at full potential (like the energy of an infant), it can then be directed to awaken the higher power centers of the body. Sexual energy, in the Taoist system, is *chi*, moving at a greater quantity and speed than normal.

The meditation begins by sitting on the edge of a chair with the feet parallel, legs comfortably apart, also parallel. The spine should be erect with the head centered; the hands are clasped palm to palm in a relaxed manner, resting on the upper thighs. The feet serve as a "grounding wire" and should stay planted securely on the floor. There should also be a slight forward tilt of the head, avoiding an energy block at the back of the neck.

Next, allow a few deep easy breaths to settle the system and begin to focus the mind. It is good to shake out any tension spots. Then, after the mind has settled a bit, send the intention to rest the mind in the navel. The intention should be effortless. You can aid the mind at first by placing an index finger on the navel to help focus energy. Visualize the navel. And as an added visualization, if needed, see the navel as the center of a target and gradually see the circles of the target shrinking, getting smaller and smaller, moving inwards toward the red inner-most circle at the navel.

Rest there momentarily until a warm energy current is felt. Next, gently intend the current two inches down from the navel to the spot called the *Tan Tien*. This will have a slightly different sensation associated with it and usually deepens the meditation. After a few moments, take the energy to the base of the penis for men and to the ovaries for women. Here, the energy tends to heat up considerably. Next, take the energy to the perineum, the place between the sexual organs and the anus. Once the energy has collected, send it down the back of the legs to the center spot behind the knees, then to the bottom of the feet, then to the tip of each big toe, then back up the outside of the legs to the points behind the knees, and return to the perineum.

At this point, there are options for further circulation which should be done only after competent instruction from a meditation instructor. For now, allow the energy to return step by step to the navel center where it can be stored.

This meditation is known as *The Microcosmic Orbit* and is often taught at Tai Chi centers or Taoist Esoteric Yoga Centers in most major cities. Mantak Chia, one of the leading advocates of the system, has written a number of excellent books on the various disciplines. His book, *Awaken Healing Energy Through the Tao* (Aurora Press), is the best book on the meditation techniques I have come across. Also, women may want to read his book, *Cultivating Female Sexual Energy* (Healing Tao Books), for more specific information regarding the meditation as it applies to women.

Overall, the meditation takes 15 to 20 minutes and does not require a lotus position of the legs or special pillows or mantras or anything but con-centration. Let me also remind you of Michael Chekhov's point regarding the power of imagina-tion. You need only visualize and imagine the ener-gy traveling and in a short time the energy will begin to actually flow. I can say personally that when the energy began to circulate in my body and I began to direct it to specific points, it dramatically improved my awareness of energy channels not only in me, but in others as well.

In addition, I have maintained a healthy and youthful constitution due to my daily practice. In fact, people who knew me years ago seem astonished to see how young I am. What they do not realize is that cultivation of chi is the fabled "foun-tain of youth" that early Spaniards had heard about. They, of course, took it to mean a literal fountain and travelled the globe searching and killing for it. They, of course, never found it.

Other things to look for, besides an increase in youthful vitality, are balanced blood pressure, im-proved digestion, healthy sleep habits, clarity of taste, smell, and all the senses. Plus, a certain con-fidence develops by intimately knowing the energy system of the body and having conscious direction of that energy. This is particularly evident in sex.

For many years, I, like most people in the world, thought of sex as a pleasurable energy urge which involved complex sensual signals that built and led ultimately to a kind of goal: the climax. This goal orientation, however, has been problematic for men and a constant source of frustration for women who wanted more from sex. The classic picture of a man reaching climax and leaving the woman unsatisfied is a tragedy of modern ignorance.

Once the energy channels of the body have been cleared through meditation, the sexual act is more than racing to climax; it becomes a meditation. In a relatively short amount of time, the man can learn what is known as *ejaculation control.* This is more than mere retention; the man actually learns to circulate the energy along major meridian paths in the body—as he does in the Microcosmic Orbit. When he has mastered this technique, the man can experience a sexual climax throughout the entire body, without ejaculating sperm.

This method of lovemaking was known to the Taoist sages for centuries and was one of their secrets of longevity. According to the Taoist system, a man's life force or chi is stored to a large degree in the sperm. Loss of sperm through continued ejaculation was literally loss of life. Consider the French euphemism for the climax: *le petit mort* or "little death."

That is not to say a man should never climax or even that full retention is advisable. Rather, the man must learn the right interval of ejaculation to suit his condition and age, enabling him to control ejaculation and prolong sex until his partner reaches satisfaction. This ultimately allows for a more pleasurable and profound sexual experience for both partners.[2]

In an ancient book called *Yu Fang Pi Chuch* (Secrets of the Jade Chamber) there is a dialogue between Tsai Nu and P'eng Tsu which explains the positive results of ejaculation control:

> Tsai Nu: "It is generally supposed that a man derives great pleasure from ejaculation. But when he learns the Tao he will emit less and less, will not his pleasure also diminish?"
>
> P'eng Tsu: "Far from it. After ejaculation a man is tired, his ears are buzzing, his eyes heavy and he longs for sleep. He is thirsty and his limbs are inert and stiff. In ejaculation he experiences a brief second of sensation but long hours of weariness as a result. And that is certainly not true pleasure. On the other hand, if a man reduces and regulates his ejaculation to an absolute minimum, his body will be strengthened, his mind at ease and his vision and hearing improved. Although the man seems to have denied himself an ejaculatory sensation at times, his love for his woman will greatly increase. It is as if he could never have enough of her. And this is the true lasting pleasure, is it not?"[3]

Masters and Johnson have also recently concluded that a man need not climax every time during sex and that there are some definite advantages to not climaxing. In fact, there are several techniques they describe (primarily to help premature ejaculators) which closely parallel Taoist techniques.[4]

The primary difference between modern studies and the ancient ways is that the Taoist methods use the mind to circulate the energy, not just manipulations and retentions. During lovemaking, the sexual energy can be directed by the male to circulate from his body into the female, and she in turn can circulate it within her energy orbit and return it to the male. This *circuit* produces a healing exchange of Yin and Yang energies, balances hormones, and creates a tender sensitivity between both partners.

When the man learns how to control sexual energy and to have climaxes without ejaculation, the method can also work as a natural birth control.[5]

While there are differing opinions on the exact ratio of ejaculations to coitions, it is generally agreed that it is more beneficial for the older man to have fewer ejaculations. And as a basic guide, it is helpful to consider the words of Liu Ching, a Taoist master of the seventh century written about in a book by Chang Chan entitled *Longevity Principles:*

> In Spring, a man can permit himself to ejaculate once in three days. In Summer and Autumn, twice a month. During cold Winter one should have semen and not ejaculate at all. The way of Heaven is to accumulate Yang essence during Winter. A man will attain longevity if he follows this...[6]

What this means for an actor is a gradual command of sexual energy that can be utilized in his craft. Not only will the actor have more energy and enjoy improved health, he will no longer be divided by the compulsive distractions of his animal nature. Most of all, he will have discovered a way of harnessing the lower functions in order to awaken the higher spiritual centers.

However, to employ this method of lovemaking makes it necessary to have a partner who is interested in sexual communion serving a higher function. The right partner is vital.

Couples who have an interest in this can consult some of the books out on the subject, but I personally suggest getting instruction from a Tai Chi Master or a Master of a living spiritual tradition. One such Master, Da-Love Ananda, in his book *The Eating Gorilla Comes in Peace,* has a chapter on the subject he titles "The Regenerative Sexual Response." In it he states:

> When the couple separates, the male should commonly or frequently retain an erection, and the female should remain full of Life and even desire. The remaining desire and Fullness is our advantage, our true food...Such fullness is itself a means of attracting more Life, whereas exhaustion or conventional degenerative 'satisfaction' only provides a means whereby we are emptied of Life in every moment of living.

And later in that same chapter:

> The regenerative process does not eliminate the orgasm; it transforms the orgasm. Thus, the response that would otherwise produce the orgasm must continue to be present in sexual communion. Through right participation in the ecstatic or overwhelming pleasurable response, something occurs in the body that is regenerative and that serves the awakening of the higher functions of the brain.[7]

In the tradition of Tantric Yoga (Tantra meaning "method"), there are *asanas* or *Yogic Postures* specifically designed for sexual union. These postures help to channel the energy along exact routes with a force so powerful it will liberate what is called *Kundalini* or *The Psychic Current.*[8] However, Tantrism (at least for Westerners not raised in Indo-Asian traditions) is highly ritualistic and although proven effective, seems, as I have stated before, impractical for Western actors.

In my experience, extensive ritual is not necessary to master ejaculation control. Others I have spoken with agree that it is largely a matter of knowing it is possible and then applying a few techniques. The only obstacle to this becoming a widely known practice is the same as the obstacle to all spiritual practice, namely ignorance. People are reluctant to sacrifice the instant roller-coaster thrills of their habitual existence in favor of slower, more subtle pleasures. What they do not realize is that these subtle pleasures are keys to unlocking energy reserves of immense power which are then used to serve true purpose and meaning in life. What could be a greater thrill?

So far I have concentrated on the male aspect of ejaculation control. Of course, women participate with the men in this process, especially in the beginning. They also benefit from the *Microcosmic Orbit* meditation, creating and circulating what is called *Ovarian Energy*. A woman can also recycle her sexual energy in much the same way a man does, with exactly the same benefits. She must learn the art of the *Orgasmic Draw* whereby she can transform the aroused sexual energy into a total body orgasm. This energy is circulated along specific routes which maintain healthy glandular and hormonal secretions and stimulate the awakening of higher energies which can be used to serve the highest spiritual aims.[9]

Female and male, both can benefit from the proper channeling of sexual energies. For the actor or actress who masters the techniques there are numerous benefits: radiant health, sexual clarity (no longer being a victim of lust), mental clarity, renewed youthfulness and vigor, a strengthened neuro-muscular system, and the cultivation of true love in the form of spiritual wisdom.

I dare say that if more people would learn to employ these relatively simple techniques, actors as well as non-actors, the world would be a much safer, more loving place in which to live.

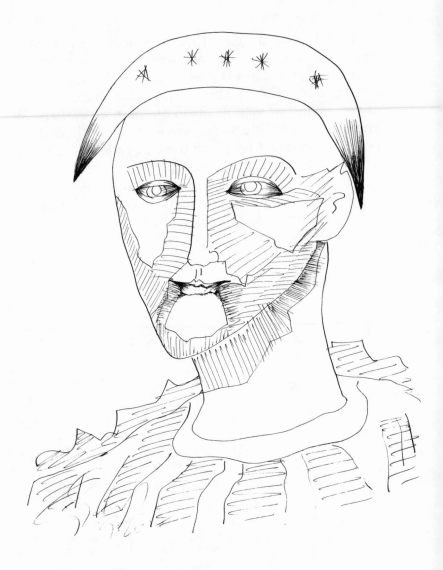

E.J. Gold, *Anatomy of a Troubadour,*
Pen & Ink, 11" x 15", Rives BFK, 1987.

CHAPTER TWELVE

DUALITY AND THE MEASURING OF PROGRESS

Since the work of Stanislavski, there has been an ongoing debate among actors and acting schools, on the subject of *Inner to Outer* versus *Outer to Inner*. That is: does an actor find truth by developing his inner work which then expands to fulfill the outer demands of the role, or does an actor work on the outer manifestations and through that, find the inner truth? The debate is best exemplified by the contrast between the generally accepted American inner to outer work and the British outer to inner. In reality, the debate carries on needlessly, because most really good actors simply do what works for them and always according to the demands of a particular role.

Not surprisingly, the world of spiritual work has a similar duality. There are those who advocate deep inner reflection which will produce results in action and behavior. Others insist that rituals and religious behavior will induce deep inner reflection. This is similar to the dual approaches to Buddhism: Zen eschews complex ritual in favor of getting first to the ground of pure consciousness and then slowly exploring other realms of mind. Tibetan Buddhism goes down gradually, exploring all the while until the ground of pure consciousness is reached, and then comes up swiftly.[1]

In the Greco-Roman era there was the famed Stoic/Epicurian debate. Stoics led a life of discipline and hard, no-nonsense inquiry into the nature of life. Epicurians led their lives on the philosophy, *live it up, for tomorrow you may be dead.*

There are examples of this duality in all levels of contemporary life which parallel dualities in religious life. On the one side there are the ascetics, living an austere and highly disciplined life. On the other side, there are those who believe that abundance, prosperity, and sensual joy are the natural expression and reward of religious purity.

A further extension of this duality exists in the idea of *redemption.* The Christian view holds that man's soul is complete and saved from damnation through his devotion and acceptance of Christ whose sacrifice insured that the family of Christians would be lifted to Heaven everlasting. There is also the contrasting view that man's soul is unformed, that the work of Jesus and others like him was a symbolic example of a process we will all have to complete in order to overcome the cycle of incarnations and to move on to our next stage of evolution.

Emotion in performance and in religion is another topic which lives in duality. According to some schools of thought, to emote and fully release emotion is good. In performance, it verifies the depth of feeling and the raw, naked truth. In religion, it verifies true surrender or forgiveness and is a meaningful show of love. The other view holds that to emote in performance is to be swept away from the event, to cloud the delicate communion with the audience, and in effect, rob them of their opportunity to emote. The comparable religious belief holds that emotionalism is not healthy, that it is a sign of impurity and spiritual imbalance.

We are again close to the dualities of psychological acting versus non-psychological acting; technique versus instinct; reincarnation versus no reincarnation; death as the end and death as the beginning; and so on.

The whole topic of *ego* is also fraught with duality. Does an actor wed or shed the ego? What about a spiritual teacher? Aren't they supposed to be egoless? Yet, why do so many of them appear to have such huge egos?

With all this duality, it's hard to know how to know if what you know is what you think you know. What is the measure of spiritual progress? If you cry because of empathy for someone else's pain, is that progress or pathology? If you get skinny or fat or no physical changes occur, is that somehow a sign of spiritual progress? What about dreams? Newly discovered powers of concentration? Losing a job or gaining a job? Sudden good fortune or sudden misfortune? What's the yardstick here?

This judgement is a primary function of a teacher. Usually, much of what a novice values as progress is either useless or a deterrent to real progress. It is like a parent helping a child. The teacher (parent) observes the learning of the child (student) and sometimes sees the child get sidetracked, or start in a direction where danger lurks and must quickly redirect the child. A mother, for instance, rarely lets a toddler wander alone towards a set of stairs.

On the other hand, a good teacher, like a good parent, knows that *always* cleaning up the spilt milk will not teach the child to clean up spilt milk.

Aside from teachers, every tradition has its guideposts, signs along the way that help to assure the seeker that progress is being made. The signs, although similar in some ways, vary from tradition to tradition.

In the Taoist tradition, for example, a sign might be the body becoming more delicate and supple, or the mind having a deep calm. Psychic powers are also a sign; however, in Taoism, as in all other paths, the so-called "powers" exist in the realm of time, and the ultimate goal is to reach beyond time.[2]

Also, from what I have gathered, regardless of the tradition, there is a moment for every seeker that signifies the point of no return. The world of ordinary phenomena begins to shift slightly and to allow a number of possible occurrences: luminous beings may appear, voices may be heard, hallucinations of various proportions might occur, along with flashes of deep emotion, involuntary movements of the body, and periods of emptiness.

Although the above conditions are often auspicious signs and a verification of spiritual progress, they might also signify the start of the *Dark Night of the Soul,* the mystic condition about which St. John of the Cross writes so eloquently. At this stage, it is important to take heed and seek appropriate help.

Obviously, this requires giving special attention to the kinds of help available and the aim of that help, and further requires the maturity to realize when help is needed.

Living in the realm of duality, as we do, is very hard on the soul which longs for unity. True progress is a state of being and in the advanced stages the usual sources of measurement, borrowed from the world of duality, no longer apply. The soul must wrestle with the dragon of the rational mind. If victorious, the mind must reform within the context of an entirely new orientation. The elements of true progress, then, may not always appear rational, nice, or acceptable.

Helping or being helped during critical growth spurts is very important. And that, in part, is the subject of my next essay.

E.J. Gold, *Heaven and Hell*, Pen & Ink,
11" x 15", Rives BFK, 1987.

CHAPTER THIRTEEN

WORDS OF WARNING

I don't know about you, but I grew up thinking that if I was nice to people, obeyed the ten commandments, and did good deeds in my life, when I died I would automatically go to heaven. That was enough. I never really questioned heaven, because I knew it had to be better than the descriptions of hell. Later, during adolescence, it was popular among my circle of friends to scoff at the notion of any kind of existence beyond death. We live and die and that's that. Big deal.

Then, after a number of extraordinary experiences, the nature of which convinced me that reality was more than what everybody said it was, I decided to educate myself. It was clear that most of my public school teachers had other things on their mind.

Drawing away from the consensus view gave me new eyes. I began to see the desperation in the faces of adults who seemed to be running, trying to escape something. I saw gaping holes in our knowledge of reality and wondered why, after all this so-called evolution, there was such rampant stupidity in the human race.

And then I wondered about heaven. I tried to imagine being totally happy sitting on a cloud in heaven, and it irked me. When I began to ask questions, I soon discovered to my great dismay that nobody knew what was going on or what we were supposed to be doing here on this planet.

Gradually, and after considerable faltering and bumbling, I was led to sources who helped me to understand what the poets and mystics were trying to communicate. Even a few of the biblical tales began to make some sense. I was guided from mystery school to mystery school, weaving in and out of theatre and the spiritual paths until a tapestry of truth began to form. As part of this, I came to know with undeniable clarity that nothing is as it seems. To step into the world of spiritual evolution is to enter through the looking glass into realms where the rational mind has no foothold.

Everyone recognizes that the spiritual path is all about transformation. But most people do not realize the amount of work needed to transform. It takes courage and fortitude to awaken. (The biblical phrase, "the meek shall inherit the earth", may very well be true. Those souls who are too meek to transcend, may be destined to remain.) That is why I have chosen to include a few words of warning. That way, when things get hairy, you can't say I didn't warn you!

The basic ground of spiritual fortitude is energy. It takes a lot of it to sustain one through the trials and tribulations of the path. That is why it is important to start early in life; later on, despite all the best intentions, there may not be the energy to accomplish anything.

Also, let me warn you, not only are things not what they seem and great resources of energy needed, but there are sacrifices that must be made. Not of the bleeding goat variety, although that would seem easier at times. I mean of the personal and very basic kind. For an actor, ambition and personal gain are perhaps the first to go.

Conventional ideas of success will be sacrificed as well. The idea of "making it" must not be allowed to dominate the energy charge of the body. Instead, a new flow of energy that *makes it in every moment*—has patience, endurance, and unlimited resources—will emerge. The fame and fortune carrot will dissolve in favor of the *feast of the now.*

The fixed self-image will have to be sacrificed. The courage to enter new avenues of learning, to risk looking foolish and to give up the need to be treated as special are all a part of this.

Friends and family are often sacrificed. Not cruelly, but they must not be allowed to deter you from your true aims. They are respected and loved as always, but as you change and grow, they must be willing to allow it fully or else they must be temporarily dismissed.

There are preparations and appropriate timing in the sacrifices, and they differ slightly from tradition to tradition. Yet, without them, the heart cannot be clear. The clinging lower self will dominate and distract you from the highest aims. It is important to note that sacrifices are made at every phase of the journey, including ultimately the sacrifice of the powers that may have accumulated.[1]

The character of the various sacrifices, plus the continuous focus of attention used in acting, the refinement of the nervous system, the radiation of audiences, and proper instruction, can lead one to the brink, the breaking point, or what in the Sufi tradition is known as *The Corridor of Madness*.

You see, part of the problem with humanity is the fact that we are wired wrong. The polarity between the headbrain and the sacral (sacred?) nerve ganglia at the base of the spine was somehow reversed. This usually happens early in childhood and is probably a result of the shift from God's will to self will. The result is a headbrain that wants to do all the mentation and a tailbrain that tries to command the movements of the body.

Through a variety of means, seekers work to return the reversed polarity to its original form. This is the famed *rising of the Kundalini energy*. What most adepts aren't prepared for is the transition period. This is a state of being produced by the process of repolarization. It is neither the consciousness of before, nor the consciousness that will be there after the transition. It is the state of being "shattered" by divine energies where the beliefs and mental constructs of the past are breaking down through the non-dualistic truth of the heart. From the outside, it appears as total lunacy. For a detailed and fascinating account of this phenomenon, read Gopi Krishna's *Kundalini,* Shambhala Press, 1971.

As a result, there is a new movement in psychology called *Psychosynthesis* which is developing methods of helping people through this difficult stage of development. Years ago, people in this condition would have been diagnosed as simply psychotic and treated accordingly. But this is changing. Some people are beginning to see the disintegration phase as necessary for a successful reintegration. In his book entitled *Psychosynthesis,* Roberto Assagioli, the leading proponent of the new movement, says this:

> Man's spiritual development is a long and arduous journey, an adventure through strange lands full of surprises, difficulties, and even dangers. It involves a drastic transmutation of the "normal" elements of the personality, an awakening of potentialities hitherto dormant, a raising of consciousness to new realms, and a functioning along a new inner dimension.
>
> We should not be surprised, therefore, to find that so great a change, so fundamental a transformation, is marked by several critical stages, which are not infrequently accompanied by various nervous, emotional and mental troubles. These may present to the objective clinical observation of the therapist *the same symptoms as those due to more usual causes,* but they have in reality quite another significance and function, and need very different treatment.[2]

One recent example of the corridor of madness was divulged by André Gregory, theatre director and title actor in the two-person film by Louis Malle entitled *My Dinner With André.* In the film he goes into great detail describing a time in his life that was full of inexplicable synchronicity, hallucination, and wild uncontrollable behavior resembling schizophrenia. He thought he was truly going crazy, only to discover later that it was a spiritually transformative process he was going through.

Another example is mentioned in *The Asian Journal* by Thomas Merton, the Trappist contemplative monk. In it he tells of an interview he had with Kalu Rinpoche, in Tibet. During part of the discussion about the initiation of Tibetan hermit monks, the Rinpoche tells him about a period in the two-year dzogchen contemplation when the initiates must encounter and contemplate the "terrifying deities."[3]

We are all familiar with the inspired madness of painters like Van Gogh, Salvador Dali, or Mark Rothko. We listen with awe to the compositions of Beethoven, Mozart, or Stravinsky, read the poetic insights of Emily Dickinson, William Blake, or James Joyce, and marvel at the inventions of great sculptors, architects, and even rock stars. Artists from all ages tend to go to the edge of their consciousness and lean into the corridor of madness, hoping not to fall. Some fall and some do not. They all, however, if capable, bring us glimpses of their vision.

St. John of the Cross, one of the greatest Christian mystics, entered the corridor and wrote of his experiences in his book *The Dark Night of the Soul*. In it he gives some directives on how to cope with the various stages. One of the first is an explanation of why such a corridor exists:

...If a soul aspires to supernatural transformation, it is clear that it must be far removed from all that is contained in its sensual and rational nature. For we call supernatural that which transcends nature, so that the natural is left behind. The soul must completely and by its own will empty itself of everything that can be contained in it with respect to affection and volition, in such a way that, regardless of how many supernatural gifts it receives, it will remain detached from them and in darkness. It must be like a blind man, finding its only support in dark faith, taking it as its guide and light, and leaning upon none of the things which it understands, enjoys, feels, and imagines. And if the soul does not make itself blind in this manner, remaining in total darkness, it will not attain to those greater things which are taught by faith.[4]

Note his insistence on detachment, even from the "supernatural gifts." Later he gives more specific warnings against attachment to mystical events that might otherwise seem all too important:

...spiritual persons not infrequently experience the presence of forms and figures that are representations of persons from the life beyond, such as apparitions of certain saints, of angels and demons, or certain phenomena of light of extraordinary splendor.

...He then, who has a high regard for such sensed phenomena errs greatly and places himself in great danger of being deceived. To say the least, he will block his way to spirituality. For, as we have stated, there exists no proportionate relationship between all these corporeal things and the things of the spirit...The reason for this is that if God produces any corporeal vision or any other sensory perception, or

if He wishes to communicate Himself to the inward-
ness of the soul, the effect is felt in the spirit instan-
taneously, without even giving the soul time to
deliberate whether to accept or reject such communication.[5]

Throughout his book he relates a progression
along the corridor, full of warnings and advice. Near
the end, he talks about the soul walking securely
through the darkest parts because it is free of diver-
sions:

The sensual and spiritual desires are now put to
sleep and mortified so that they can no longer enjoy
the taste of any Divine or human thing; the affections
of the soul are restrained and subdued so that they
can neither move nor find support in anything; the
imagination is bound and can no longer reflect in a
rational manner; the memory has lost its strength;
the understanding is in darkness, unable to com-
prehend anything; and hence the will too, is in
aridity and constraint...It is in this kind of darkness
that the soul, according to its own words, travels
securely. For, when all these operations and movements are arrested, it is evident that the soul is safe
from going astray. And the deeper the darkness is in
which the soul travels and the more the soul is
voided of its natural operations, the greater is its
security.[6]

It is possible to work alone, to progress steadily
amid the chaos of the world. At some point, however, it may become necessary to find help. And be
forewarned, once the corridor is entered, there is no
way out except by way of the other end. Early exits
from the corridor almost always end in madness.
That is why guidance and help during this major

transition stage is such an important function of a mystery school.

Yet, even within the relative security of a school, there are, from time to time, casualty cases, people who entered the corridor only to lose their way. This is rare, but a possibility and a risk nonetheless.[7]

The sixties saw a great number of casualties due to the indiscriminate use of psychoactive drugs and Yogic practices. Fortunately, the escapist motive has dwindled somewhat in seekers, and that contributes to a more responsible approach to spiritual work.

Therefore be forewarned. The spiritual path is not for dilettantes. An actor of great depth and dedication can recognize that part of himself which occasionally calls out for mediocrity, whispers things like "oh, it'll do" or "we'll live with that." As it is fatal to the artist, so too those whispers are fatal to the seeker. *Getting by* is simply unacceptable.

And know from the outset that although spiritual practices may enhance certain aspects of one's art, they do not supplant hard work and true aptitude. One must not make the mistake of adopting a spiritual quest in order to fulfill artistic ambition. Spiritual progress does not automatically make a good actor.

Also, beware of *spiritual pride.* This is a common malady in young seekers who do not know enough to know how much they do not know. They often give "expert" advice to friends and family without the slightest notion of the consequences. In some, the pride manifests as the exaggerated mask of humility; their outward presence is completely humble, but inwardly they strut with pride and self-love.

Beware also of turning spiritual practice into parlor games. Those people who like to dabble in such matters are meddling in areas where they do not belong. The actor is a vehicle, a tuning fork, if you will, and must assume a responsible position by studying slowly and carefully under the appropriate guidance.

Books that encourage indiscriminate healing for the sake of healing or astral projection for the sake of astral projection (or worse for the sake of science), for example, do so out of naive enthusiasm for those powers. Unfortunately, they are dangerously ignorant of the consequences and aims of such powers.

My advice, again, is to find authentic instruction. The old adage, *seek and ye shall find,* still holds true. There are guides and teachers available. One's perceptions and readiness will lead one to the guide most suited for the particular stage of development. Then the journey can begin with a secure foundation.

One final word of warning. In Itzhak Bentov's book, *The Cosmic/Comic Book,* he develops an equation that warns of developing *Will* before *Love.*[8] I agree. One's love nature should be strong and unsentimental, providing the steering force for the will. The development of true love through sacrifice, service, devotion, prayer, contemplation, or whatever means, can then direct the will as it develops to serve the highest aims. If done the other way, one risks being seduced by the powers and falling prey to the lure of personal gain.

The world is full of men and women of power, who abuse their power for political or social gains. These black magicians often do not recognize their abuses. They assume that their power is a God-given right. True spiritual transcendence, however, is generated from love and in directions unconcerned with temporal power. Let your true heart feelings be the guide.

E.J. Gold, *Strange Angel*, Pen & Ink,
11" x 15", Rives BFK, 1987.

CHAPTER FOURTEEN

CHANNELING

Oh for the wonder that bubbles into my soul,
I would be a good fountain, a good well head,
would blur no whisper, spoil no expression.

What is the knocking? What is the knocking at the door
in the night? It is somebody wants to do us harm.

No, no, it is the three strange angels.
Admit them, admit them.

—D.H. Lawrence

We are currently experiencing a massive resurgence in communication with the invisible realms. It has progressed at an exponential rate lately, due to the efforts of celebrities like Shirley MacLaine and the occasional notoriety of some of the Channelers.

The difference in today's movement is that it is a phenomenon that is crossing over all previous boundaries of social, religious, and financial station. It shows signs of being a truly collective step.

This event harkens back to previous "spiritualist" movements, many of which ended in scandal. Exceptions notable for their integrity are people like Alice Bailey (who by the way coined the phrase "New Age"), Edgar Cayce, and Jane Roberts.

For decades, the information and abilities of these psychics have fascinated and baffled sceptics and believers alike. Now it seems they were pioneers in a growing field where currently an unprecedented number of people, claiming to have psychic connections, are channeling entities and information from the beyond.

Some say that channeling is only snake-oil showmanship, while others swear by it and live their lives according to advice gained from these psychic transmissions. Numerous books and tapes have come out on the market, including a directory that lists over 500 channelers. And that's not counting the hundreds more who for various reasons remain "underground."

There is no denying it; in one form or another, channeling is becoming a component of our spiritual framework. Personally, I suspect it always has been. The New Testament is supposedly "channeled" through the various authors who compiled it after the death of Jesus. Shakers, Quakers, Baptists, and a wide array of evangelical Christian religions believe in "getting the spirit," some even to the extent of "speaking in tongues."

Polytheistic religions have long ago made their peace with the occurrence of channeling. In India, for instance, where ritual theatre is still very alive and functional for the people, when an actor portrays the god Rama, the audience knows without a doubt that Rama is present. In this sense, the actor is channeling the god, much like current trance channelers who are channeling an entity.

Therefore, I perceive religious worship, theatrical ritual, and channeling as essentially variations on a theme. They all use certain laws which make extradimensional communication possible, precisely as the shaman does. In religion, the congregation is asked to banish its disbelief and to worship its God. In theatre, the audience is asked to banish its disbelief and identify with the action onstage. In channeling, the channel is asked to banish his or her disbelief and open the self to higher entities.

In all of these examples, people choose to see or experience something as real, thereby opening up to a new reality. Theatre, then, becomes very much like what the contemporary composer John Cage uses as his definition of theatre: "Theatre is made by using one of two frames: either by the viewer looking at a subject 'as theatre' or by performers 'intending to make theatre.'"[1] In both examples, there is a conscious choosing to focus the attention and define the new reality.

In a seance, there must be a medium, a person whose psychic instrument *has faith,* can tune in and be transported to, or receive the transportations from, other realms. Acting as the tuning mechanism of focused attention, the medium goes into a trance where the invoked spirit can impinge upon the teleceptors and the kinetic functions of the instrument.

A good actor, therefore, like Thespis, is a good medium. Through preparation and refinement, the actor can invoke high spiritual energies in the roles of gods, heroes, and saints. The actor can invoke slightly lower energies in the form of struggling or non-struggling mundane humans. Slightly lower we see clowns, buffoons, and idiots. Lower still, we see cruel murderers and violent, ugly people. Even lower we meet demons, gargoyles, and beasts.

Of course, a good actor knows that most characters are invoking a fluctuating frequency depending upon circumstances. Reflecting the truth of the human condition, a character may be a beast one moment and a hero the next. The actor, therefore, is there to show us how we are usually entranced by life, helplessly invoking a confusing array of energies and becoming the pawns of our own powers.

At the same time, the actor demonstrates through the act of acting the ability of humans to cease unconscious identification with the energies by taking conscious control. This gives hope for humans to be able to dehypnotize themselves from their compulsive, limited views of the world. It further establishes a means to respond to their higher aims.

In his book, *Between Theatre and Anthropology*, acclaimed theatre researcher and director Richard Schechner says:

> We might even say that there are two kinds of transportations, the voluntary and the involuntary,

and that character acting belongs to the first category and trance to the second. However, having watched trance—and having seen many films depicting it—I suspect that the differences between these kinds of transportations have been overemphasized. The character actor is self-starting (at least if he has orthodox Euro-American training), but once warmed up and in the flow of things, he is deeply involved in what Keats called the "negative capability," and what I've schemed out as the "not me-not not me." The character actor in flow is not himself, but he is not not himself at the same time. Also, trance performers are frequently conscious of their actions even while performing them; and they too prepare themselves by training and warm-up. The difference between these kinds of performance may be more for labeling, framing, and cultural expectations than in their performance process.[2]

Like a chant or a mantram or a koan, the actor's repetitions of the script and of the voice and postures of the intended character, during the development of rehearsal period, work on the telepathic circuits of the brain. In a moment similar to states in meditation, an actor feels a *shifting* or a *clicking in* and the character seems to be fully there. Robert DeNiro and Meryl Streep are famous for their abilities to "plug in" as it were to their characters. This is very much the same process as that of a trance, the key elements of which are: alignment of inner and outer postures, tuning to a psychological outlook, adopting new rhythmic sensibilities, and the all important *leap of faith.*

In free-form improvisation, this leap happens first and the attributes of character follow the flow of the character's needs and desires in the unfolding situation and the needs and desires of the other characters in the scene (a lot like ordinary life). In a more structured improvisation, a good actor only deviates from the scenario when he or she is "hot" or "connected" and this governs the flow of the improv (like life during occasions that are familiar scenarios). In both cases, the actor is playing with the lightning-fast shifting of inner states and outer manifestations, tuning in to characters that have a *working persona.*

That is what we use every day. However, our normal working personas have been formed through socialization, gratification of sensual pleasures, and dependence on others.

Every situation in life at some point calls forth the appropriate mask, automatically and uncontrollably. The real self will eventually recognize the discrepancy between its wishes and the tyranny of the masks which make it feel trapped. This is the beginning of despair.

The Buddha declared that one of the primary sources of our human despair was the belief in a fixed self, which according to his doctrine does not indeed exist. He hoped to teach others about the *beingness that precedes the construction of the selves*—the true being that is transcendent, beyond the concerns of the personality.

The personality was perceived by the Buddha as a conglomerate invocation of masks. If that is so, then who is wearing the masks? According to Buddhism, it is the Buddha—we are all Buddhas, temporarily hypnotized by the magnetism of our masks.

Like fighting fire with fire, the actor whose essential self recognizes the dilemma can fight masks with masks. He can consciously invoke his masks, going deeper and deeper into the process until he has no fixed persona.

En route, one must find the inner master, the one who is conscious of the changing masks. The source of truth and the strength to face life without a mask comes from this master within.

One way to begin contacting the master within is to use a form of channeling I call the *inner improv.* Getting to the liberating aspect of the master is like peeling an onion. Layer upon layer must be experienced and the peeling process is not altogether enjoyable. This exercise is designed specifically for actors and can be especially useful for actors who have had contact with a spiritual teacher.

At first, it is a free form experience. I suggest creating a workspace that evokes a special atmosphere. This could be as simple as clearing a room or putting candles on a table. Whatever works. It need not be solemn. It is just a way to signify clarity of purpose.

Next, place about the room in various locations books that are inspirational to you. Also put a few notebooks around with pens next to them. Put a few special garments in various places. These garments should represent qualities of "the master." And finally, create a throne or power place where you can sit or stand and speak from your heart of hearts.

Then, having cleared two to three hours of uninterrupted time in the space, knowing also that you cannot be overheard by anyone, begin to improvise. Walking about and rambling out loud at first will start the ball rolling. Picking up an inspirational book and reading from it at random further focuses the event and keeps the thoughts flowing in the right direction.

Remember to be playful, allowing yourself to be as outrageous as you want. Also remember, you are searching for the "master" within yourself, the one who *knows,* so be sure to *ask questions.* When an answer starts to come, be attentive to where it comes from.

Be careful not to preconceive the master character. Keep in mind that a master need not be entirely stern or always of the same sex. Experiment with master characters who are demanding or funny or provocative or even silly at times. Let many manifestations come to the surface. Edit nothing!

Out of these free-form sessions will begin to emerge a character or several characters that speak from a very deep place within you. They will sometimes startle you with their lucidity and insight. And very often they will have unusual and highly unique mannerisms. When you get to this stage, begin to keep a tape player going with plenty of blank tapes to use. Just turn on the tape and record, for hours if need be.

For actors who have studied with a master teacher, it sometimes happens that the teacher's mannerisms and voice can be mimicked until the teacher seems to be speaking through you. Of course, what has happened is those manifestations have unlocked the inner master that the teacher represents to you.

As always, discovering what you do know brings to light what you do not yet know. The inner master can help to clarify intentions and with the new-found vision of what needs to be learned help to formulate a true aim. By this I mean formulating a plan of what needs to be done to discover what remains unknown. Then, once the plan is clear, a personal vow (a deep unbreakable vow) is made to carry out the plan for the benefit of all sentient beings. Having an aim will galvanize the resources of your soul and greatly enhance your chances of evolving in this life.

I have included an edited transcript of one of my inner improv sessions as an example of how the inner improv works and the value that might be gained. As you will see, this session came out as a classic dialogue format: questions and answers. Other formats, however, have proven to be just as effective and useful.

In this one, I played the character of the Student (S) to my Inner Master (M).

Very little has been changed from the original recording. This particular exchange took place in the late evening during the peak of a three hour session.

THE MASTER WITHIN

S: Master, I barely know where to begin on this...I know time is of the essence and I am still filled with questions. With the limitations of time, I—

M: Do not hesitate with talk of time. What are your next questions?

S: OK, as far as I know, I have been struggling with the dual aspects of my path: artistic survival and spiritual understanding.

M: Yes,...so? There is duality within each duality.

S: So, yes, well...my questions are really an attempt to create an aim, you know? Some true target for my life that will help me to get on without useless distractions.

M: OK, I'll buy that. So?

S: Well, in the work...a...of awakening, of...well, in almost all profound spiritual practices, the seeker is guided towards detachment and impartiality. How can a man be a performer and be impartial?

M: (Laughter) I knew you'd ask me that. You are really responding to your own fear and mistrust of the success machine. This is good. Success and fame can only work to keep you asleep. You wish to awaken, yes? Or do you want to live your life asleep, bouncing from here to there, from right to left, not having any decisions, not having true happiness; always searching, grabbing, money-hungry? You want to live like a machine? Then, fall into the success factory. You canna fall inna...inna, looka me now, I'ma dooina bad Italian accenta! No good! In any art form there's a way. Do you think Zen mindfulness applies only to flowers and arrows? It is in everything. It is in massage, martial arts, painting, poetry, music, theatre, and on and on and on. It is in listening. It is in every moment as it unfolds. Being with the moment. How can you be with the moment if you are being somewhere else? Having a conversation cha cha cha with yourself; fighting within your mind, "Should I do this? Should I do that?—Is this my real life? Is that my real life? What is dream about? This book? This, This This!" Chatter! And you haven't asked yourself the true question. So then you come to me and want answers? You feel the need to talk to your true self.

S: Yes. All of this is true. And I also feel the need to talk to others. I have made some discoveries. I have been working. I haven't been totally asleep. Often I think of that scene in the film *One Flew Over the Cuckoo's Nest* when Jack Nicholson goes over to the sink and tries with all his might to pry it from the floor in order to smash it through the window and free himself. Everyone else in the room just stares at him. I was genuinely moved by that scene because I saw that moment as a metaphor for so many other moments in my own and everyone else's life. And I thought about the kinds of theatre and entertainment that is usually offered and it all seems diversionary. As if somehow it was contrived to support only the linear, rational point of view. As if our dreams, our ecstatic moments are reduced to taboo. Especially in America, I sense there is no audience for conscious or ritual acts of art.

M: Yes, this is partly true. And not only in America. Art has many levels of creation and consumption. It is also in the digestion that the artist is found. In your digestion. Where are the artists of audience—the artistic audiences who know how to digest what they have been served?

S: And that brings me to another question, education.

M: What about another question? I say something real and all of a sudden you burst with questions. What do you want from me? All right. You
want to talk about education? What is that?

S: Well, most education side-steps the real issues
of birth, death, consciousness, and so forth. I have
recently been teaching in the academic world and
sometimes I feel...strange. I don't know. I guess I'm
asking, "Is it right to be a seeker and a teacher all at
once?"

M: You can do no real harm. Unless you begin
to assume power roles. Learn how to seal the space,
how to protect the space for the student to learn;
how to read the student; how to inspire loyalty—not
to you, but to your art. Learn to make true inspiration. Learn how to light the fire of learning and how
to repair the body. Most important, use the challenge to observe yourself!

S: Yes, I have at times tapped the observer and
know how strong a force it can be. Especially in times
of stress. But I find it very difficult to use at home.
My wife and I are work partners. We practice
numerous meditations, do Tai Chi, keep each other
alert to inner movements and inner revelations. But
what do we do about role distortion and anger...you
know, the typical teeter-totter effect?

M: Teeter-totter? What do you mean, teeter-totter?

S: It's a playground toy. When one side is up, the
other is down and visa-versa.

M: Ah yes, I know this toy. Well, the ups and
downs mustn't become an energy thief. It is a subtle
trick of the sleep machine. If a partner has anger, you

must strive to understand. Try even to put on their shoes; to have compassion for their suffering.

S: Yes, but what if it seems unreal...I mean, it may be real to her or to me at times, but the other might recognize it as a conditioned response.

M: Open your heart...listen. Allow the organism to vibrate in harmony with that other organism. Not to damage the essence, just to listen. So it must not be an identification with the emotion. Yet you mustn't remain cold or aloof. Too much detachment, too early, is unwise until the relationship is on another level.

S: What about planning...I mean the aspect of planning where to live, to work, to grow, etc. has been a constant distraction. Do we plan or just let the spontaneous moment lead the way?

M: Yes.

S: I see, I think.

M: Therefore you are?

S: Right! Descartes before the horse. I'm sorry for that last literary leap. I'll continue—

M: No, you can continue with your literary leaps. You want to leap literarily...literally with your literary and literal translations, then your litany is literary, continue!

S: OK, I'm going to ramble a bit here—

M: Fine. Ramble if you want to Mr. Rambo rambling. You can shoot your thoughts down one at a time. You can get in your own war in your own head. Let them tumble out; from garbage in to garbage out.

S: OK, so far I grasp the situation like this—

M: It's important for you to grasp situations isn't it? To grasp! You Americans are always holding on to things. Go on, grasp away.

S: OK, we are souls, magnetically assimilated into this realm as part of some unknown process. I say magnetically because most of our beingness, most of our awareness, is electromagnetic; synaptic flashes from patterns of chemical—

M: I understand magnetism—who do you think you are talking to? Continue, continue!

S: Right. OK, certain aspects of the human process point towards evolution, towards a reformed humanity; towards a reunion with the creator. It seems that in every spiritual tradition, be it monotheistic, pantheistic—

M: The *is* stick? Do you hit people with this stick of is? Oh, sorry, you are waiting on me now aren't you. Go on, continue, continue! This is fun!

S: All right. Now, the human process points towards evolution, a reformed aspect of humanity—

M: And reunion with the creator. Yes, get on with it. Go Go Go!

S: (Flustered) a...right..There are three basic aspects to the human sphere; that is, organic life of course, plus a functioning aspect that mixes into a blend of an active creation/destruction cycle that—

M: An act of creation? Only God makes acts of creation. You don't create yourself unless you are God. You are, that's it. You simply are. It's a blessing. You are here and then you are not here. You go from one room to the next, but what you do in this room is important and you have to finish this room before you go to the next. So you must be here in this room, yes?

S: Right.

M: Right.

S: I am trying to be in this room. It's just the thoughts—

M: Yes, I know, the thoughts, the theologies, the is stick, the dots. You're having dots and they are swimming in your mind. And you need to pull them together into one big dot. Then you'll be a big dot...how about dat? (laughter) Continue, continue! Let's talk. This is fun!

S: There seems to be a presence within the organism which observes. And this, according to most teachings, has only three attributes: presence, focus of attention, and adoration. Usually these attributes wander willy-nilly, being swept into the carnival of the senses. When detached, however, the consciousness can de-magnetize itself and remove itself from the organic maelstrom, preventing hypnotic involvement in emotions. It can live in several dimensions at once. And that brings me back to my earlier complaint about the one-dimensional aspects of most contemporary performing arts—

M: Careful, you're preaching again. Get to the point. Let's go, let's go.

S: All right, it has adoration, presence, and focus of attention and it wants to grow...so it grows in other dimensions. It is then subject to other laws. When the adept can function in both worlds, then he or she can work to either remain in the next world or come back and guide others across the river. The opportunity to do such a thing depends upon overcoming a very powerful current. Most are swept away, to be reborn into circumstances formed purely from accumulated habits; often wallowing in sleep for many lives, unaware that there is a river, a current that can be crossed.

M: My butt hurts...enough for one night.

S: No wait, please. Just a few more questions.

M: Well, we'll change postures a bit—stretch. Start again soon when you actually have a question, hummmn? (After a short break) Now, let's continue with these interesting insights and so-called questions.

S: OK. As an actor, I get a lot of positive feedback and I can sense the moments when I am connected...but a lot of it makes me feel so absurd, so useless and even counterproductive. Am I to assume that acting isn't really part of a spiritual path?

M: Be careful of assumptions. You say it feels useless. Well, what is more useless than a beautiful sculpture or painting? Or a poem? Counterproductive? Well, it's possible. First, there are many paths; you must learn to take the information you have and separate it from knowledge. What is it that you *know?*

S: Well, I know that there is a lot that I do not know.

M: Good! That's a start. You can say, "I don't know this," so you can start to formulate what you actually *do* know. What else?

S: Well, I know my body pretty well. I can, for example, achieve deep calm if I focus my mind or meditate.

M: Yes, and?

S: And the movement of chi or prana...well, when I tune in to the flow, it is a warm and comforting feeling. I know there are these moments...like when I am performing and I mirror someone, the moment becomes elastic and completely beyond thought. I have had similar experiences while learning a new task of some kind. I have also had rare dream awakenings when the dream becomes lucid and the content leaves me with a profound resonation.

M: OK, that's good. Let's stop there. You had a dream revelation. What do you know about the energy of a dream?

S: Well, I recognize the difference between a dream I am observing and a dream in which I am actually there, fully involved; even to the point of manipulating the dream. I saw my hand once in a dream, and that brought on an amazing rush of energy in my body.

M: That's it? That's all you know about dreaming?

S: I remember images from what I call my *message dreams.* One in particular has since influenced my search.

M: Aha. And if you continue to search, is there still the need for the dream? Should you release it?

S: Well, it pointed me in a path that seemed to go from—

M: From here to there, from there to here, from here to here. Wherever you are, you must at least be here. Are you here?

S: Yes.

M: Are you sure?

S: Yes!

M: Yes? Good, prove this.

S: I am speaking to you.

M: You can't possibly be totally here if you are just speaking. What else?

S: I don't know...it's the only proof I have.

M: That makes me a little sad. (silence) So, when you get your information from dreams, or from me, or wherever...what form does this come to you? In what form does your knowledge transform?

S: Well, in a theatrical form usually.

M: Hence this form we are in, yes?

S: Yes, exactly.

M: Hmmmmmn. So you have met a triangle of masters. You have brushed a school. The moth comes to the flame. You read many source books, utilize techniques, risk change...it's good. But you must grow towards the light. Like a plant by the window, growing, growing, in this direction...but someone must come to turn the plant sometimes; otherwise, the plant will be imbalanced, deformed...one-sided.

S: (pause) I think I have enough to digest for today.

M: No, we go on. Your butt hurts? So, one more point. A.....what was it?

S: Could it be—go back to your art? That everything I really need to know is in my art? Yes...I...well, dammit, what is my art?!

M: I see. You have many talents, many interests. You do not know which interest to follow. If you are an artist, what is it that dictates your artistic interest?

S: The form of expression?

M: And?

S: And the inner search.

M: So, what is an artist?

S: Someone who in some way contacts the inner forces and tries to reconcile them to this world through forms of expression?

M: You are asking me?

S: But I dabble in so many things! I am like a child set free in a toy store. I want to paint, to act, to write, to meditate, to mime, to photograph, to do so much.

M: Yes, this is America and you have the freedom to do these things. Sometimes it is a confusion. Too many things. But there is joy in this dilemma, yes? So why the confusion?

S: I feel the necessity for an aim. For one thing— one single, simple thing.

M: Why can't you be happy to be a Renaissance man? To do many things? Do them well and give them your full attention. You must juggle like the fool; a creative fool...like the fool in the Tarot cards. You know this? What is this image?

S: Well, he's a comical character near the edge of a cliff and there is a dog barking at his heels.

M: Yes, and with him he has only a small bag— for small possessions. Essentials! He has his head up high and risks falling off the edge. But at least he goes to the edge! He walks that line. But eventually you must do the same. You must find your own unique way of walking to the edge while moving in the world. This cannot emerge while you are trying to please Mommy or Daddy or the system. You must have the courage to—

S: I know, to live without answers.

M: To work for them! Not by plunging into layers of social status, but through seeking in your work, your silence, your inner music, your awareness.

S: What about compassion?

M: What about it?

S: Well, to tell you honestly, I get so wrapped up in myself, I become a small, insular package. I suspect myself lately of not having any true compassion.

M: That may be true. But it is better to be true than to have false love. But if you had no compassion, why would you invent— why would you create?

S: Well, I want to have compassion; to love.

M: Or be loved? Are these seductions? You want to seduce love your way?

S: Well, yes...sort of.

M: What is it you want from this love?

S: I don't know. I really don't. I suppose *home.* I guess I am hoping to find home.

M: And what does this home look like, what does it feel like?

S: I see having a home as a sort of hermitage, a retreat in nature with—

M: What is the feeling? I don't care about the carpentry skills in your head. What is the feeling?

S: Warmth. Joy in my heart. A closeness to others. A sense of progress on a path; of being able to measure progress.

M: Good. But this is a lot of ego talking too, you understand. You want to be seen as holy, as warm. This is what you are projecting. The impulse is within your deeper wish for freedom. Try not to romanticize your life. Keep trying to ground yourself in reality.

S: You know, I think I have a serious problem with reality. I mean, there are so many realities to deal with. And then fear creeps in...I have this fear of violent or vulgar manifestations both in myself and in others. I am moody and sullen at times for no apparent reason. It's stupid.

M: Be careful not to use your criticism as another extension of self-obsession. Also, you speak of Compassion or Love—you must not limit these with definitions. What are the experiences of love you have within your current reality?

S: Well, I love my wife, but—

M: But, what? What is the love?

S: It is a kind of deep mystery, a respect. I mean, when I sense our connectedness or even in moments of distance, it's all a part of those moments when I realize the universe is truly alive. I sometimes freeze with awe at these moments. To suddenly feel, not just have the thought, but to *feel* that I am on a planet that is spinning in a vast universe of stars and that I am in a relatively fragile container; a container made up of smaller containers made of still smaller ones and on and on. In those rare moments...it's hard to explain....I just feel a deep shame.

M: Yes, perhaps you should. But don't worry, you must hold this shame. It is a precious substance. Let it lead you to more and more awareness. This process might open for you the true meaning of love. Listen, we are living in a time of very rapid change. Consciousness is evolving very quickly and many changes are in store. As we grow, there are so many more avenues of inner awareness open to us—competing for our attention. Do not be overcome with confusion. To meet and transcend this confusion is the artist's chief work; not only for his or her benefit, but for the benefit of all. Transmit the simple message of the heart. No more separation. Love is the energy that drives the artist; inviting others to participate in the miraculous journey from the world of matter to spirit—if it matters to you. And if it does, that means there is work to do, yes? Enough for now.

E.J. Gold, *The Matador's Woman,*
Pen & Ink, 11" x 15", Arches, 1987.

CHAPTER FIFTEEN

PRACTICAL EXERCISES

The following exercises can be useful in experiencing directly the parallel facets of spiritual work and actor training. They should be approached with lighthearted simplicity. With the exception of the "Life Review" exercise, which is private, they should be done by groups of five or more.

It is important to follow each one of these exercises with a non-judgmental and informal *assimilation session*. During the session, each participant should have the opportunity to express verbally to the entire group his or her subjective experiences regarding the exercise. Having the opportunity to speak about the experience helps to solidify the changes that may have occurred and bring to light certain aspects that may be common to everyone.

Remember to keep in mind the acting focus of each event and make sure to include that perspective during the assimilation session. These exercises should indeed be treated as *events*, having the potential to awaken profound and life-altering insights in one or all of the participants.

It is not advisable to attempt more than one of these events in a 48-hour period. They will need time to reverberate in the being and take a place in each person's body of experience.

Also, they should only be done in a closed, clean space; free from clutter and interruptions. Always start with a group warm-up that invigorates and prepares the breath, the body, and the voice.

Some exercises are useful in making discoveries beyond the individual. Very often there will arise a new appreciation between members of the group, resulting in a more authentic ensemble spirit. That is why some exercises are more directly applicable to the rehearsal process than others.

Above all, these exercises should be done gently, without pressure to arrive at a predetermined result. Let them unfold naturally and in accordance with the group chemistry. Beware of participants wanting to use the event to lead the group towards their own personal manipulations for attention. Make it clear to everyone, beforehand, that it is a *group* exercise and they should leave their personal baggage outside the workspace.

It should be noted that the proper use and consequently the results of these exercises is entirely the responsibility of the leader and the participants. Use them well and they will unfold to reveal deeper and deeper layers of truth.

CHILD'S EYES

The leader may participate in this one as long as someone watches the time. Allow a full half hour for this event. It is best done in silence. Because of the nature of the interaction, this one is very useful in "bonding" a group, especially before a rehearsal or performance.

To start, have everyone stand in a relaxed, centered posture and gently pat their relaxed "tummy." Use the image of the "two-year-old tummy" open and unguarded. Then have everyone massage their own tummies clockwise with the palm of their left hand flat on the belly and the right hand on top of the left. (In this instance, clockwise means if you look down at your own belly, the 12 is just below the navel while the six is just below the sternum). Have everyone sigh long easy breaths to further drop the belly.

There may be some unstressing reactions such as giggles or yawns; this is fine during the early stage. Later as everyone continues to relax, the faces should open and stay free of expression, and people get in touch with their simple two-year-old mind. As this begins to happen, everyone should simply look about the room, enjoying colors and textures.

Next, they should begin to walk with a simple easy gait, not trying to "put on" a baby walk, just walking simply. Gradually they should begin to encounter one another and look into each other's eyes. When this begins, it is important for the leader to do a bit of side coaching.

Quietly the leader reminds them to keep their tummies open and relaxed; if they perceive any tension creeping in, they should use the observation to let it go. The leader should ask them to keep their thoughts open and relaxed by saying:

"Look at those eyes you are seeing and with the simple curiosity of a child, ask yourself, 'who's in there?'"

The leader might spend a few minutes softly reminding participants to drop their armour more and to slow down as sometimes a group will rush the eye contact. After awhile, the leader can rejoin the group.

Gradually, the group will arrive at a very serene and yet powerfully connected place. The participants should try to spend at least three minutes in continual eye contact (more if need be). If it is a large group, the event can go to 45 minutes.

Generally, the rule is to try to have a good contact with everyone in the group. Naturally, in a large group of ten or more, this isn't practical. If it is allowed to go too long, the eyes will become fatigued and the mind will become agitated, undoing what had been established.

Break the silence with a few voiced sighs and let everyone stretch a moment and rest the eyes. After a few moments, sit and review some experiences. If this has been done several times with a cast, however, the talk afterwards is unnecessary.

MOVE TILL YOU LAUGH

This exercise is a great warm-up and a super inhibition breaker. The leader should step out of the work arena for this one to act as ongoing side-coach.

At first, the leader commands the group to move until they genuinely make themselves laugh. The group will inevitably start off way too wild and big and a lot of forced laughter will be heard. After a moment or two, the leader should stop everyone and remind them that the movements need not be huge, in fact tiny movements may evoke laughter just as well. They should all remember their private moments when they catch themselves doing something absurd or silly. Then with a quick command, they should begin again.

The leader this time just shouts over the din, reminding them to move until they get a *genuine* laugh. The leader should encourage the group with a few "Yes that's it!" and "Go for it, come on!" and any other phrases that boost the group's ability to let go.

There will usually be a peak moment when lots of real laughter is heard. Certainly the movements will be unusual and very hilarious. This is a great exercise to prepare a group for comic characterization and to invoke the light comic spirit they need before a comic performance.

Before long, the laughter will begin to sound wooden again and at that point, the exercise is over.

TIME TRAVELLING

This is one of a number of "threshold exercises" I have used to help actors access their *will center*. It is very demanding and should be done with the utmost seriousness and care.

This one does require music. I often use very slow, melodic harp music to give the room a gentle ambience. Participants should be dressed comfortably and warmly, no jewelry or junk in pockets. A sweat suit or dance attire is ideal. I suggest bare feet as well.

The leader does *not* participate in this event. In fact, it is useful to have an assistant, especially if it is a large group (10 or more).

The event should happen in a secure spacious room, preferably on a wood floor. Concrete or carpeted surfaces are difficult for this event and should be avoided if at all possible. The room should be at a comfortable temperature with proper ventilation.

To begin, following a short warm-up, everyone will lie down on the floor on his or her back, leaving ample room between each other. Keep the music going throughout. And remind the group that they should go to the restroom before they begin. There's nothing more frustrating than doing this exercise with a throbbing bladder. Then, the leader should lead the group through a few deep breaths, to settle the system and focus the mind.

Although directions were explained beforehand, the leader should once again reiterate what they are about to do: they are asked to go from their prone position to a standing position in a *slow* and *continuous* manner. The slow is extremely slow—the slowest they have ever moved! It should take two hours to stand completely.

It is important to remind the group that their movements are to be continuous, flowing, and slow. Even their eyes, tongue, and facial movements should be very slow.

If it happens, and it often does, that they find themselves in a bind, they must solve the problem with the same slow movement.

To make it easier, I have on occasion demonstrated a simple trajectory that will save them a lot of steps. From the prone position, I first roll my head to one side, then my opposite arm comes across my chest and my opposite knee lifts and crosses, effectively putting me on one side. I then struggle to free the arm under me. Next, I maneuver myself to all fours, separate my feet and slowly rock back into a squat position. From here, and with my head hanging, I lift the buttocks, straightening the legs, and eventually roll up the spine.

Everyone is different. Each will inevitably find personal variations on that trajectory, but it will at least provide a pattern to follow if they get in a super bind. Speaking of binds, once in a while someone will get the body into a real doosie of a position and because of the placement—because a shirt is obstructing the mouth, or whatever—he or she needs assistance. The leader and the assistant should keep watch for such situations and offer only the necessary help to get the person back on track again. Keep in mind, there is much to be learned by the obstacles encountered on this slow journey, so don't feel obliged to save them from themselves.

Although gruelling at times, the exercise is also filled with amazing and very rewarding aspects. For one, the participants come face to face with their little angel that says, "Aw, go ahead, you can cheat a little here—no one will notice"; and even more important, they come face to face with the will center which demands accuracy and honest work effort.

There is a psychic level to the event as well. The slow movement seems to put the mind into orbit. Memories, dreams, voices, and all manner of mental phenomena start to unfold, creating additional struggle for the participant, working to maintain the intention to stand at the same slow, continuous pace. It helps if the leader says slowly and softly some of the following phrases every ten minutes or so:

"Resist the temptation to go fast."

"Stay slow, you have all the time in the world."

"Keep your focus here in the room—going from this position to a stand."

"If you get in a bind, reverse at the same slow pace and try another solution."

"Don't forget to breathe."

Before beginning, make sure none of the participants are dealing with an injury or illness.

Diabetics or even borderline diabetics should not do this exercise.

The leader is also the timekeeper and should tell the group when they are 1/4 finished, 1/2, 3/4, and then nearing the two hour mark. Of course, everyone does not have to finish at two hours. Some will finish earlier, some later. Impress upon the group, however, that they should make it at least to the 3/4 mark.

When they come to a stand and as the head lifts, the leader or assistant should whisper to them to take a few steps and then gradually find a chair and sit down. The assistant should have ready some cups of water for everyone and some kleenex for those who are releasing emotionally. There are occasions when a participant needs a kleenex during the work, and I have as the leader simply held the kleenex to the nose and done the honors without too much fuss.

The effects of the time-travelling event vary widely. Some participants burst into tears, others feel a deep peace, others feel powerful—like they could run a marathon—and some are just plain pooped. All of them however, have a new awareness of themselves and a renewed confidence in their abilities.

They will also, no doubt, have experienced time as an elastic or liquid concept, no longer exerting a rigid stronghold on their awareness. By experiencing this new state of being (and it is definitely an altered state), the participants are given a new reference point for their sense of time. Changing their relationship to time can endow them with new pos-

sibilities and the will to accomplish their highest
ideals.

This event should not be done more than once
in any three day period. As an added challenge, the
time-travel should be longer, if only by five minutes,
each time it is done. This is very demanding work,
so it must be treated with the utmost care and
respect.

THE MESSIAH

There is a teaching in the Kabbalah (the mystical
Hebrew tradition), originally introduced by Rabbi
Isaac Luria in the sixteenth century, that perceives
the concept of the Messiah not as the coming of a
person, but as a symbol of world harmony.

Legend has it that Luria gathered his disciples
one Sabbath evening and told them he could bring
the Messiah that very Sabbath. He made it clear that
there must be complete harmony between everyone
throughout the duration of the Sabbath. They were
not even to have the slightest confrontation. This
they did until near the end; a trivial argument broke
out which escalated to a disagreement between two
disciples. He later explained to them that because of
their weaknesses, Satan had worked again to create
disunity and forestall the Messiah.

The following exercise uses this premise to create an improvisational situation that can help activate new levels of characterization. This is a
variation on the Hebraic theme whereby the characters gathered are not disciples at all, in fact they are
total strangers. Inherent in this fact is a certain ten-

sion and distance between the various types of people. Their task then is to establish, for at least one minute, complete harmony.

What happens is this: each person in the group arrives "in character." How the characters are developed is up to the class. (In my classes, this exercise is used after the students have completed at least three weeks of character research and development). They should know their characters well enough to remain in character, respond and react in character, and immerse themselves in the scenario in character for at least an hour.

Once all the characters have arrived, the leader welcomes everyone and in a pleasant manner tells them the following: "I know you are all anxious to discover exactly what you are doing here and how you came to be here with everyone else. That will all become clear as we progress. Let me first say there is no need to panic, all your needs in terms of food, air, and water will be taken care of. My superiors have instructed me not to tell you anything else at this time other than that you are asked to meet one another and get to know each other before my next visit.

"There is no need to try to escape through the door(s) or window(s) because what you perceive as solid matter is in fact nothing more than a hologram supported by your collective thought patterns. And please do not be alarmed by my sudden appearance or disappearance; this is a natural function that will also become clear to you in the near future. Until then, I bid you goodbye."

I usually snap my fingers in front of me, as if I had disappeared, and then I can step "unseen" to a chair along one of the walls to sit and observe.

A number of things might happen at this point. A lot depends on the characters assembled. Whatever happens, it is important that no one look at you or in any way allow your presence to invade their reality. They will be slow and possibly confused at first. Inevitably, the first attempts at character improv will sound terribly trite and just plain phoney. As they progress, however, this aspect improves immensely.

Characters who are natural leaders might start the ball rolling by introducing themselves to people or making a speech or investigating the room, looking for a way out. The leader should just sit by and let things take their course. After about ten minutes, the leader should snap back in and provide the next instructions. Do not be surprised if characters talk to you and want to know more than you are telling them; evade their questions as well as you can. The next instructions go something like this: "Hello again, I hope you all had enough time to acquaint yourselves with one another. My superiors have told me to inform you of your situation. Some of you come from different times and different backgrounds. The reason you all can meet here is that this is a holding chamber between realities. You are neither alive, as you once were, nor are you dead. You are at an in-between place that has no time.

"You must decide among yourselves if you want to stay here together for eternity, or return to your former lives. To return, however, takes a special effort on everyone's part. In order to dissolve the hologram, everyone here must decide upon and enact a group ritual of complete harmony lasting for at least one minute. When this is done, you will return instantly."

It never fails that there follows a burst of questions or reactions, even during the speech, so the leader should remain flexible. If a question pops up that cannot be fielded, the leader can always say he will ask his superior and then snap out of the scene to plan the next tactic.

This is when things start to heat up. Some characters are thrust into despair, others seem indifferent, some even think it's an elaborate joke. Gradually, the characters struggle to arrive at a plan of action. Of course, human nature makes it difficult for people to agree on anything and this is usually heightened by people in character. This stage can go free-flow anywhere between ten and twenty minutes, at which time, the next instruction is given: "I am sorry to have to tell you this, but there has been a change of instruction. You no longer have the option to stay here together for eternity. If you do not complete a unified ritual within the next ten minutes, you will be taken from here and killed one by one. If in ten minutes you are unable to unify, then you must decide on who will be the first sacrifice. That is all I can tell you for now. Good luck."

Now this is a little cheezy, I know. But it serves to intensify the experience. The time limit zooms everyone to action and yields some very interesting results. It is especially interesting to see how they go about finding a ritual. Or, if a ritual is not found, it is equally interesting to see how they go about selecting the first sacrifice.

At exactly ten minutes, the leader should re-enter and demand to be given the sacrifice. Unless of course they have unified, in which case the exercise comes to a halt and the actors can drop character and discuss the discoveries.

If a sacrifice is taken, the leader and the person will snap out and watch the next sequence of events. Several sacrifices can be taken or sometimes it is useful to send back the first one who relates a story of unspeakable torture and horror and tries to convince them of the importance of enacting the ritual.

If it appears that there will never be a ritual, the leader should end the improv and allow everyone to discuss the event.

The rituals themselves can be just about anything. That is part of the charm of the exercise. It's fun to see what a particular group will use to display their attempts to unify. I have done many of these exercises and only twice have I witnessed a truly unified ritual. Both times it was a struggle, but a glorious thing to see when it happened.

It may take a few of these improvs to bring the characters to full shape. The dangers involved are the characters making their moments too melodramatic or undervaluing their situation. Occasionally, I have interrupted the exercise and challenged the group indeed to place themselves in the situation, as if it were real.

Of course, as in all such exercises, participants are not allowed to abuse physically anyone else or in any way to threaten the safety of the participants. I will allow things to heat up if, for example, an argument occurs, but if it starts to build to physical violence, I yell "freeze," reminding them of their task to ride the edge of the reality, but not to fall into it.

LIFE REVIEW

This is a private exercise that can be done anytime, anywhere. All that is needed is a sincere effort to maintain a certain perspective for a specific span of time. It is a very transformative exercise when done fully and because of that, the "player" should avoid diffusing its power by talking about it.

The exercise is this: At a predetermined time of day, the player decides to alter his perspective of reality for a full hour—with no lapses. He or she, during that hour, observes and participates in life as if he or she were experiencing the *life review* which occurs at the moment of death. One believes one is dead and at the same time, part of the consciousness knows it is living.

There is a poignancy as each moment unfolds. The exercise is different for everyone and a lot depends on where one is and what one is doing. What seems universal is a sense of wanting to be the kind of person and do the kinds of things that will not make the review seem banal. Everyone reports a deepening of values and a renewed appreciation for moment to moment existence.

When people practice this exercise regularly over a period of time, they can begin to live their lives differently. Their work as actors improves immensely, and they begin to want to take their growth seriously. Most of all, there seems to be more love and forgiveness generated.

While not directly applicable to the stage, this exercise, in an indirect way, is working the muscles of observation and of the special concentration needed to maintain character perspective. Plus, with the added incentive to do quality work, there is often marked improvement on all levels of their craft.

I mentioned earlier not to talk away the energy of this exercise. By that I mean to say, avoid telling anyone what is going on during the work hour. There can be some minimal discussion in the group to clarify things and to let people validate their experiences, but for the most part, it is much more effective when done privately.

INNER ARTIFACT

This is another private exercise. It makes use of the instrument's natural tendency to form habits. This exercise can be used to create vocal, physical, and psychological characteristics that are decidedly different from one's own collection of habits. By doing this, it follows the ancient concept of "new lamps for old."

There are two ways of approaching this; both are valid. One way asks that you, the actor, while in the middle stages of character development, draw a number of abstract quick sketches that best depict the essence of the character. Next, pick one line or create a conglomerate line that seems to capture the basic spirit of the person you want to portray.

In the second approach, you examine a number of lines drawn on paper and pick one that stimulates your inner involvement. From this line, you can use this exercise to arrive at a unique characterization.

To begin, you take a fairly large drawing of the line (14 X 18 or larger), and pin it up on the wall in the work space. Once secured to the wall, the line should not be moved or altered for the duration of the session.

Next, stand in front of the drawing and without moving the body, begin to *breathe the line.* Softly inhale following the shape of the line, almost as if the line were entering the lungs. The exhale should follow the same pattern in reverse. Do this while looking at the line and listening for any inner feelings that may start to surface. This should continue, slowly and easily, for at least five minutes.

Gradually let the breath influence the movement of the head. Draw out the line with the head as you breathe the line. Let the facial features respond to the line as well. Draw with the eyes, nose, ears, tongue, every part. Keeping the breath connected to the movement, let this exploration filter down to include the shoulders, the arms, the hands, the chest, the waist, the hips, the pelvis, the knees, the ankles, and the toes.

After the entire body has had a chance to experience the line, stand still again and simply breathe it. As you do this, listen again for any feelings and let that influence the choice of what body part to move. Allow the breath to try out different tempos of the line as you explore the feeling with a single part of the body.

Begin to add the voice, softly at first. Let the voice follow the rhythm and feeling of the body. At this point, you can move away from the drawing and enter the space, allowing the movements more room and more dynamic.

As the exploration of the line continues, there may be moments of "double think" or a sudden block. If this happens, and it is not uncommon, simply go back to the drawing and re-charge with a fresh look at the line. Once the mind is out of the way again, drift into the space with the voice and movements exploring the line again and again.

Anywhere from ten to twenty minutes might pass during the initial exploration stage. You have total freedom by entering the limitation of this one single line. Going full tilt into the line will allow you to find things completely outside the realm of cliche. However, let me remind you to use common sense and avoid overstraining the body or voice.

Try not to force the exploration in a predetermined direction, let it take its own shape. Very often, during a line study of this nature, an actor will avoid going in directions that seem unrelated to the character he is working on. Keep in mind that an exploration is a journey into the *unknown* and as such should not be limited by preconceived notions of how the character is to be played. It is by having the courage to trust the uncharted territory that you can discover powerful character traits outside your personal bag of cliches.

After an unbridled exploration into the space with the voice and body, find the essential posture of the line. Exaggerate the posture and try a variety of walks still following the dictates of the line. As the body walks the posture and rhythm of the line, begin to add a few words or phrases that seem to emerge from the exploration at this stage. Do not judge the content! What you say at this point is inconsequential; it is merely a first try at opening the psychology to the shape of the line.

This next phase of exploration is critical. By now you know how the line feels inside and how it manifests in gestures, posture, walk, and breath. Now begins the absorption of the line into the being.

Stand in the center of the space and begin to breathe the line again. Gradually form a pattern of movement that is generated from the breath. The pattern should involve as much of the body as possible and should be saturated with feeling. Repeat the pattern again and again at a comfortable dynamic until there is no question as to its complete shape.

Then, little by little, the pattern should increase in size and dynamic. You will begin to use more breath, more power, more space, making it larger and stronger in regular increments. This should build vocally as well. The pattern will expand in every way until you are using the entire room and are at the maximum level of vocal and physical dynamic.

Stay only momentarily at the peak and then begin to return in the same incremental manner. Step by step, the pattern will reduce in size and dynamic until, eventually, it will return to the comfortable level at which you began the crescendo. Do not stop here though. Let the line idle for a moment or two and then begin to diminish the dynamic, internalizing the pattern gradually.

Slowly, the pattern will become minute, the breath will be extremely small, and the pattern will have internalized to the degree that it will continue inside *with no outer manifestation.* At this point, the line has become a mantram, or inner artifact, that will begin to allow the character to emerge organically, from the inside.

Gestures, speech rhythms, movements of the eyes, the breath, the laugh, the very soul of the character will follow an essential code. At first it will need a bit of effort to sustain the connection to the artifact. Later on, it need only be activated with a thought, and then you are free to go on to more spontaneous acting dynamics, trusting that the character will now follow the new line of habits naturally, and any personal habits will be at a minimum.

The beauty of the technique is that it can be activated at a moment's notice and can also be dismissed with a quick command from the mind. It is useful for all styles of acting, for all characters, and does not interfere with the actor's need to be in the moment. More than that, it establishes a deeper level of trust in the actor's creative potential.

SELECTIVE PERSPECTIVE

This exercise teaches how to locate and use an inner switching device that alters the perception and emotional involvement with the outside world.

To begin, have a group walk around the space in a random pattern of movement. Then ask them to begin to allow themselves to be irritated by what they see, hear, or perceive in any way. They can use each other or even themselves as long as they do not act this out or make it obvious to anyone else what they are irritated at.

As the exercise progresses, the participants will begin to become agitated, irritable, moody, defiant, and angry. Encourage truth by saying, "let it work on you, don't *try* to feel anything, just let yourself be irritated." Watch their bodies for honest reactions to their perceptions.

Next, direct the group to allow themselves to be charmed by what they see in others or perceive around them. They mustn't "show" what they are being charmed by; instead, they must simply allow themselves to be charmed.

This time, they will begin to smile broadly, laugh, sigh, and generally "light up." The room will have a completely different ambience. Encourage them to search for new and ever more effective charms. This usually builds to an almost unbearably positive atmosphere.

After a few moments, allowing them to experience this fully, ask them to return to a neutral state. There from neutral, discuss the things perceived that managed to affect mood. The emphasis should be on the fact that they are, in large part, responsible for how they perceive the world.

Further emphasize that this inner mechanism is the same device needed to "see through the eyes of a character". It isn't very effective for an actor to try to drum up a mood to fit his character. It is better and even easier to allow the character's perspective to produce the mood in the actor.

VILLAGE OF THE IDIOTS

This is one of my favorites, because it is so useful in introducing and playing out the fundamental idiocy of the human condition.

Start with participants on the floor, lying down on their backs. After a moment or two of relaxation, you welcome them to the "Idiots' Convention." They are all idiots at the convention and have somehow managed to get to this position on the floor. Their next mission is to get to a standing position. They must do this in the most idiotic fashion possible. Here's the way I usually narrate this—feel free to expand or improve upon it: "Now, without hurting yourself or anyone next to you, you must get to a stand in the most idiotic manner possible. There is no logic to this. It's ridiculous; makes no sense. OK...and...Go!"

Invariably, a good 50% of the group will begin doing the most outrageous and physically strenuous things possible. Let them go at it this way for a moment or two (as long as they are in no danger) and then stop the exercise to say the following: "OK, idiots, that was lovely. Except that a lot of you were using brute strength as your only means. Remember, there is no logic whatsoever. You may want to sing yourself to a stand, or borrow the help of a pet mosquito, or become a fig tree, anything! If one attempt isn't successful, go to another one. Of course, none of them will succeed; but that shouldn't stop you from trying. OK, take a breath, ready and Go!"

There is usually more invention at this stage and some of the attempts will be hilarious. I usually wait until I see a majority of interesting approaches and then yell "freeze." I then quickly ask each idiot, one at a time to continue with his or her own attempt to stand. This gives the others a chance to see the variety of choices around them and further inspires a non-rational approach. I then encourage them really to believe that their way, regardless how idiotic, will actually work for them.

After a minute or so, I tell them that their way is magically working for them, and it will indeed allow them to get to a standing position. Once standing, I tell them to greet their fellow idiots!

Next, and this is the critical adjustment, I tell them that they are in a normal world all of a sudden and that they want to try to appear normal. They must take their cues of behavior from those around them. Whatever they are doing must be "right" and "normal." I help guide this by interjecting comments like: "How are the others walking? What's the normal way to walk here?"

"How do people talk and communicate?"

"Stay alert, try to convince them that you are normal."

This follows its own course with people trying to discover the "right" way to sit down, to laugh, and to behave. It can release loads of inhibitions very quickly and helps people to see how social conditioning is a means of hiding the essential human comedy.

E.J. Gold, *Circe*, Pen & Ink,
11" x 15", Rives BFK, 1987.

CHAPTER SIXTEEN

CONCLUSION

I used the word "actor," but at a certain stage of human development the actor becomes an "agent", for he has come to realize that through him the purpose of the universe is indeed focussed according to the time and place of his life performance. The ego in him has become a crystalline lens through which the "Will of God" is concentrated into individualized acts. He does not think; the One Mind thinks him. His life has become "sacred" because it is no longer "his" life, but the Whole performing within and through the space of his total organism, and at the time determined by the rhythm of the planetary process, whatever act is necessary.[1]

—Dane Rudhyar

The human drama of life on earth is usually acted by bumbling amateurs who learn their roles half-heartedly without even recognizing what play they are in. They stumble blindly from scene to scene, stealing focus or blowing lines or missing entrances, hoping the playwright will fix things if they get in a bind. And they are always in a bind!

Then there are those humans who recognize the value of professional work. These beings study, observe, rehearse, investigate, and learn the lines necessary to get them out of the dark backstage arena and into the well lit altar of the stage.

Why should inspiration and growth in the spiritual dimension be relegated only to poets, musicians, painters, and dancers? The actor too has the right and the means to enter through the mysterious gates and struggle to awaken.

I challenge the new actor to join with the ancient actor and make even the smallest, most insipid assignment a spiritual task. Therein is the secret of overcoming the powerful current of mediocrity we now are facing. And perhaps, in time and with the help of all other workers in the spiritual dimension, there will be audiences who know how to digest what they are given. In those moments when the theatrical event is perceived as a possible vehicle of enlightenment, the art will have returned to its sacred function and actors will no longer need to "shop around" for spiritual guidance.

Until then, I suggest putting to work what can be gleaned from this text and beginning to match it with work that is in some way connected to a bona-fide tradition. Also, it can be very useful to form a group of fellow actors who are also searching for truth, and are willing to make a few sacrifices.

I do not know if the present surge in actor popularity will last. Hopefully, the flaky and sensational aspects of the craft will eventually diminish without actors losing the influence they now enjoy. The timing is critical, however, for if actors do not make the quantum leap in consciousness that other fields seem ready to do, actors in the next century will fall hopelessly into another dark period as social outcasts.

Do not allow this to happen. Take your nimble gifts and noble efforts into the crucible of the spirit. Emerge whole and clear-eyed as living examples of the new actor fearlessly participating in the full spectrum of human redemption—bringing light and joy to the hearts of many who thirst to awaken. Do this and you shall be a friend to all humanity.

NOTES

CHAPTER I—The Actor

1. Richard Schechner, *Between Theatre and Anthropology* (Philadelphia: Univ. Pennsylvania Press, 1985), p.36.

CHAPTER II—History

1. Brian Bates, *The Way of the Actor* (Boston: Shambhala Publications Inc., 1987), p.22.
2. Jeffrey Mishlove, *Roots of Consciousness* (New York: Random House, New York, N.Y., 1975), p.5.
3. Mircea Eliade, *Shamanism* (Princeton: Princeton Univ. Press, 1972), p.20.
4. Shirley Nicholson, *Shamanism,* Chapter 10 by Larry Peters—"The Tamang Shamanism of Nepal" (New York: Theosophical Publishing House, 1987), p.174.
5. *ibid.,* p.166-167.
6. *ibid.,* p.85.
7. Brian Bates, *The Way of The Actor,* p.22.

8. Fred Mayer and Thomas Immoos, *Japanese Theatre,* Trans. Hugh Young (Studio Vista, N.Y.: Rizzoli International Publications, 1977), p.38.

9. *ibid.,* p.38.

10. *ibid.,* p.38.

11. Jeffrey Mishlove, *Roots of Consciousness,* p.22.

12. Richard Schechner, *Between Theatre and Anthropology,* p.134-5.

13. Plato, *Five Great Dialogues,* Trans. B. Jowett (New York: Walter J. Black Publishers, 1942), p.31- 65.

14. Jeffrey Mishlove, *Roots of Consciousness,* p.23.

15. *ibid.,* p.23.

16. Peter Brook, *The Empty Space* (New York: Athenium Books, 1968), p.65.

17. Russell Zguta, *Russian Minstrels* (Pittsburgh: Univ. of Pennsylvania Press, 1978), p.101.

18. *ibid.,* p.111.

19. Peter Brook, *The Empty Space,* p.62.

20. Frances A. Yates, *The Occult Philosophy in the Elizabethan Age* (London: Ark Paperbacks, 1979), p.70.

21. *ibid.,* 89-126.

22. *ibid.,* 159-163.

23. Elenor Fuchs, "The Mysterium: A Modern Dramatic Genre", *Theatre Three,* Journal of Theatre & Drama of the Modern World (Carnegie Mellon Univ., Fall 1986), p.73-86.

24. Leo Shaya, *The Universal Meaning of the Kabbalah,* Trans. by Nancy Pearson (Baltimore, Maryland: Penguin Books Inc., 1973) p.61-73.

CHAPTER III—Stanislavski, The Mystic Realist

1. P.D. Ouspensky, *In Search of the Miraculous* (New York: Harcourt Brace and Jovanovich, Inc., 1949), p.105.

2. Constantin Stanislavski, *An Actor Prepares,* Trans. by Elizabeth Hapgood (New York: Theatre Arts Books, 1936), p.123.

3. Constantin Stanislavski, *On the Art of the Stage,* Trans. by David Magarshack (N.Y.: Hill & Wang, 1961), p.164.

4. *ibid.,* p.169.

5. Ouspensky, *In Search of the Miraculous,* p.106.

6. Stanislavski, *An Actor Prepares*, p.187.
7. *ibid.*, p.187.
8. Constantin Stanislavski, *Building a Character*, Trans. by David Hapgood (New York: Theatre Arts Books, 1977), p.60.
9. Stanislavski, *An Actor Prepares*, p.271.

CHAPTER IV—The Tao of Acting
1. James N. Powell, *The Tao of Symbols* (New York: Quill Press, 1982), p.124.
2. Benjamin Hoff, *The Tao of Pooh* (New York: E.P. Dutton Inc., 1982), p.10.

CHAPTER V—What Is Going On Here?
1. Itzhak Bentov, *Stalking the Wild Pendulum* (New York: Bantam Books, 1977), p.25-56.
2. *ibid.*, p.38.
3. *ibid.*, p.31-33.
4. Ouspensky, *In Search of the Miraculous*, p.181-198.

CHAPTER VI—Sleep and the Awakening
1. Brook, *The Empty Space*, p.50.
2. Jerzy Grotowski, *Towards a Poor Theatre* (Denmark: Odin Teatrets Forlag, 1968), p.216.
3. Daniel Goleman, *Varieties of the Meditative Experience* (New York: E.P. Dutton, 1977), p.56.
4. E.J. Gold, *The Human Biological Machine as a Transformational Apparatus* (Gateways/I.D.H.H.B. Publishers, 1985), p.45-46.

CHAPTER VII—Higher Bodies
1. Bentov, *Stalking the Wild Pendulum*, p.135-139.
2. Hua-Ching, Ni, *The Taoist Inner View of the Universe and the Immortal Realm* (The Shrine of the Eternal Breath of Tao Press, 1979), p.142-149.
3. *ibid.*, p.144.
4. P.D. Ouspensky, *In Search of the Miraculous*, p.180.
5. Bates, Brian, *The Way of the Actor*, p.175-178.

CHAPTER VIII—Higher Purpose

1. Z'ev ben Shimon Halevi, *Kabbalah and Exodus* (Boulder: Shambhala Press, 1980), p.43.
2. Bentov, *op. cit.*, p. 184.

CHAPTER IX—Mindfulness

1. Lama Anagarika Govinda, *Creative Meditation and Multi-dimensional Consciousness* (New York: Questbook, Theosophical Publishing House, 1976), p.125.
2. Thomas Merton, *The Asian Journal* (New York: New Directions Journal Publishing, 1973), p.300-302.
3. Edward Marsel, *The Resurrection of the Body—The Essential Writings of F.M. Alexander* (Boston: Shambala Press, 1969), p.11-26.
4. *ibid.*, p.8.
5. *ibid.*, p.58-59.
6. *ibid.*, p.116.
7. Merton, *The Asian Journal*, p.401.
8. Brad Darrach, "Meryl Streep—On Top and Tough Enough to Stay There" (*Life Magazine*, Dec. 1987, Volume 10, #13), p.72-82.

CHAPTER X—Gateways

1. Ni Hua-Ching, *The Taoist Inner View of the Universe and the Immortal Realm*, p.68.
2. Halevi, *Kabbalah & Exodus*, p.199.
3. Michael Chekhov, *To the Actor* (New York: Harper & Row, 1953), p.12.
4. Ajat Mookerjee and Jadhu Khanna, *The Tantric Way* (London: Little, Brown and Co., 1977) p.23.
5. Halevi, *op. cit.*, p.200.
6. Fred Gettings, *The Encyclopedia of the Occult* (London: Rider and Co. Ltd., 1986).

CHAPTER XI—Sexual Energy and Acting

1. Elizabeth Haich, *Sexual Energy and Yoga* (New York: Aurora Press, 1972), p.36.
2. Jolan Chang, *The Tao of Loving* (New York: E.P. Dutton, 1979), p.29.

3. *ibid.*, p.21.
4. *ibid.*, p.41.
5. *ibid.*, p.111.
6. *ibid.*, p.43.
7. Heart Master Da Love Ananda, *The Eating Gorilla Comes in Peace* (San Rafael: The Free Daist Communion and The Dawn Horse Press, 1987), p.331-345.
8. Mookerjee and Khanna, *The Tantric Way*, p.26.
9. Mantak and Maneewan Chia, *Cultivating the Female Sexual Energy* (New York: Healing Tao Books, 1986), p. 177.

CHAPTER XII—Duality and Progress

1. Merton, *The Asian Journal*, p.265.
2. Hua-Ching, *The Taoist Inner View of the Universe and the Immortal Realm*, p.86-106.

CHAPTER XIII—Words of Warning

1. E.J. Gold, *Autobiography of a Sufi* (I.D.H.H.B. Publishers, 1977), p.114-118.
2. Bentov, *Stalking the Wild Pendulum*, p.224-225.
3. Merton, *The Asian Journal*, p.165.
4. St. John of the Cross, *Dark Night of the Soul*, Trans. Kurt Reinhardt (New York, Frederick Ungar Publishing, 1957), p.33.
5. *ibid.*, p.47-48.
6. *ibid.*, p.207.
7. E.J. Gold, *The Joy of Sacrifice—Secrets of the Sufi Way* (I.D.H.H.B. and Hohm Press, 1978), p.33.
8. Itzhak and Mirtala Bentov, *The Cosmic/Comic Book— On the Mechanics of Creation* (New York: E.P. Dutton, 1982), p.43.

CHAPTER XIV—Channeling

1. Schechner, *Between Theatre and Anthropology*, 248-249.
2. *ibid.*, p.127.

CHAPTER XVI—Conclusion

1. Dane Rudhyar, *An Astrological Mandala*, (New York: Vintage Books, 1974), p.34.

ABOUT THE AUTHOR, MARK OLSEN

A self-described "cosmic snooper," Mark Olsen has a solid background both in professional theatre and on the spiritual path. He attended Trinity University in San Antonio, Texas, where he studied acting with Paul Baker, well-known Dallas Theatre Center Director who created the productions *Hamlet ESP* and *Journey to Jefferson,* the dramatization of Faulkner's *As I Lay Dying.*

After his college acting career, Mark left the mainstream acting approach to study with Kabbalist mime teacher, Samuel Avital. Olsen toured as a solo mime performer, delighting audiences throughout the country. He learned also in New York from the stage direction and shaman's theatre-craft of E.J. Gold, transformational psychologist, author, artist and performer.

As a successful mime, Mark Olsen went on tour world-wide with the acclaimed European mime/mask troupe, Mummenshanz. Subsequently, he returned to the professional stage in roles such as "Renfield" in *Dracula* and "Charlie" in *The Foreigner,* at the Victory Theatre in Dayton, Ohio. Olsen also investigated experimental theatre by studying with Moni Yakim, Director of the New York Pantomime Theatre and Movement Instructor of the Julliard Conservatory Theatre School; and the Roy Hart Theatre in France, which has specialized in "vocal archaeology" and developed remarkable techniques of dramatic projection.

Mark Olsen's spiritual training began in his Arizona childhood with the influence of Native American ceremonies. Aside from theatre work with the demanding teachers, Avital and Gold, he studied martial arts with Taoist master Don Ahn, trained in the Zen Buddhist tradition, and learned the esoteric lore of Christian and Hindu mysticism. With this in-depth inner investigation as an integral part of his life, it is no surprise that Mark insists on combining self-development and universal ideals with his stage practice.

Currently a respected educator in the theatre field, Mark has taught theatre at Ryerson Theatre School in Toronto, Carnegie Mellon University, Antioch College, and the New York Open Center. He currently teaches acting at the Acting Academy in Cincinnati, Ohio, and coordinates the acting program at Wright State University in Dayton.

Mr. Olsen's published articles include the following:

"The Metaphysics of Stage Combat", *The Fight Master*, January, 1988.

"Three Gentle Masters Speak", *The Whole Life Times*, Jan/Feb 1984.

His teaching is the subject of an article by Stephen Policoff entitled, "The Elusive Aha!", *New Age Journal*, March, 1985.

Mark Olsen's first book, *The Golden Buddha Changing Masks*, is the culmination of years of investigation in the acting and spiritual disciplines. The author offers his book to students, actors, and all other "cosmic snoopers." For Mark, it is an integral part of his service to fellow seekers—especially fellow seekers in performance careers.

INDEX

Letter to the Reader:

Gateways is pleased to present for you Mark Olsen's first book. We are sure that he will continue to write books sharing his ideas and his practice in theatre training. We hope to continue publishing his work for you, the interested reader, whether you are a theatre professional, an initiate on a spiritual path, or simply an adventurous reader.

If you wish to contact Mark regarding his current workshop and lecture schedule—or his availability for any training event related to the ideas in *The Golden Buddha Changing Masks*—write to him c/o Gateways at the address given below.

Gateways also produces an extensive line of high-quality books, audio tapes and videocassettes. Their subject matter is practical spiritual work, transformation, and advanced coursework both for inner awakening and for artistic applications of these ideas.

For a current catalog, don't hesitate to write or call us at the following address/phone:

Gateways Books & Tapes
PO Box 370-GB
Nevada City, CA 95959

(916) 477-1116